India
the Eternal Magic

ISBN: 81-7437-025-0

Text: Antara Dev Sen © Lustre Press

Published by
Lustre Press Pvt. Ltd., 1995
Revised edition 2000
M-75 GK Part II (Market)
New Delhi 110 048, India
Tel: (011) 6462782, 6442271
Fax: (011) 6467185,
E-mail: roli@vsnl.com

Conceived and designed by Pramod Kapoor
at Roli CAD Centre

Jai Kumar Sharma: Map (page 18)

Photo Credits

Amit Pasricha: Pages 12-13, 56, 57
Avinash Pasricha: Pages 8-9, 96
B.P.S. Walia: Pages 24-25, 68-69
Dheeraj Paul: Pages 28, 29, 39, 53, 93, 94
D N Dube: Page 92
Ganesh Saili: Pages 21 (bottom), 91
Hemant Mehta: Page 31
Kalyan Chakravarti: Pages 80-81, 83
Karoki Lewis: Pages 52, 66-67
Krishna Deo: Page 19
Lustre Press Library: Pages 1, 2-3, 4-5, 10-11, 20, 21 (top), 22-23, 27, 30, 33, 34-35, 36, 41, 54, 55, 60, 62-63, 64, 65, 72, 73, 77, 82, 85, 90, 95, end paper
Pankaj Rakesh: Pages 16-17
Pramod Kapoor: Pages 6-7, 37, 58-59, 86-87, 89
Sanjay Singh Badnor: Page 79
Sondeep Shanker: Page 78
S Paul: Pages 42, 50-51, 74-75;
Fotomedia:
Thakur Dalip Singh: Pages 14-15
Dinesh Khanna: Page 61
Amit Pasricha: Front Cover

Printed and bound at
Star Standard Industries Pte. Ltd., Singapore

India

the Eternal Magic

ANTARA DEV SEN

Lustre Press
Roli Books

Sitting in a hand-pushed trolley, an official inspects the railway line—the changing face of the Kangra valley against the timelessness of the Himalayas.

Immortal love, immortal beauty—a breathtaking view of the Taj Mahal from the central fountain. One of the seven wonders of the world, Shah Jehan's epic creation—the Taj Mahal—lives to tell a story of unparalleled love.

Classical Indian dance is said to be poetry in motion. But more than the rhythm and lyricism of traditional India, the classical style from the Northeastern state of Manipur reflects the cult of Vaishnavism. The love of Krishna gives Manipuri dance enormous freedom of expression, ranging from the exquisitely mellow to the daringly jubilant, where the miridangam marks time.

A spectacular view of Jaipur at sunset, from the ramparts of Nahargarh . . . as far as the eye can see. Nahargarh was the summer retreat for the zenana or the women's wing of the palace.

Goa offers a strange mix of Portuguese and Indian cultures, set in the lap of nature's luxury. Washed by the Arabian Sea, it flaunts the best beaches in the country. One usually finds what one seeks in these magnificent stretches of sand and sea, whether it is solitude, tranquillity, beauty or just pure fun.

The Golden Temple or Darbar Sahib, Amritsar, is one of the most important shrines of the Sikhs; every Sikh aspires to go there at least once in his lifetime. The shrine houses the original copy of the Granthsahib—the holy book—which is taken out in a procession on special occasions.

Built by Rana Kumbha in the 15th century, Kumbhalgarh, a few miles from Udaipur, is one of the most important forts of Rajasthan. And like most of the forts of the Mewar region, it is haunted by the memories of chivalry and self-respect, where death was chosen over dishonour. Which often led to the mass suicide of Rajput women in the ritual of jauhar, *as the men rushed out to meet the victorious enemy in a fight to the finish.*

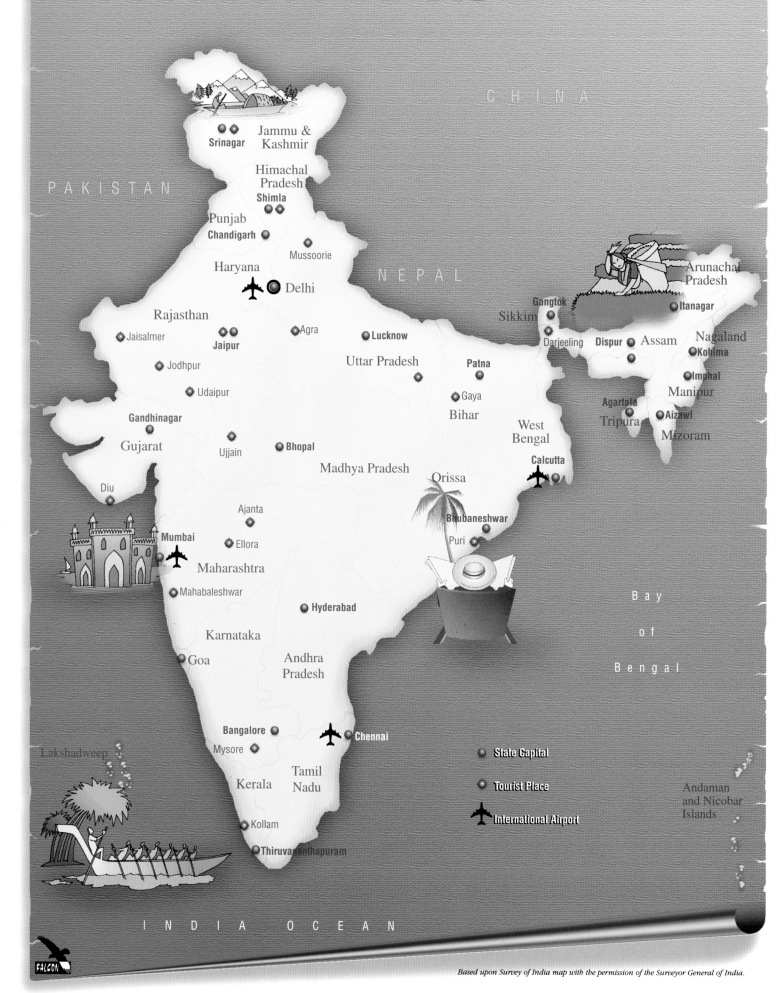

INDIA

CHINA

PAKISTAN

NEPAL

Srinagar

Jammu &
Kashmir

Himachal
Pradesh

Shimla

Punjab

Chandigarh

Mussoorie

Haryana

Delhi

Rajasthan

Jaisalmer

Agra

Jaipur

Jodhpur

Lucknow

Udaipur

Uttar Pradesh

Patna

Gandhinagar

Gaya

Gujarat

Ujjain

Bihar

Bhopal

Diu

Madhya Pradesh

Orissa

West
Bengal

Calcutta

Ajanta

Gangtok

Sikkim

Darjeeling

Arunachal
Pradesh

Itanagar

Dispur Assam

Nagaland

Kohima

Imphal

Agartala

Manipur

Tripura

Aizawl

Mizoram

Bhubaneshwar

Mumbai

Puri

Ellora

Maharashtra

Mahabaleshwar

Hyderabad

Karnataka

Andhra
Pradesh

Goa

Lakshadweep

Bay

of

Bengal

Andaman
and Nicobar
Islands

Bangalore

Mysore

Chennai

● **State Capital**

◇ **Tourist Place**

✈ **International Airport**

Kerala

Tamil
Nadu

Kollam

Thiruvananthapuram

INDIA OCEAN

Based upon Survey of India map with the permission of the Surveyor General of India.

FALCON

1
The Birth of a Nation

It was midnight. And as is to be expected at that hour, there was hardly any clarity of vision as the tricolour unfurled atop the parliament building. There was just a hazy vision of the future, as the Union Jack was rolled up and stashed away forever, as thousands lent their voice to *Jana Gana Mana*, the song that was beginning its life as the national anthem of an independent India. There was a vision of a secular country, proud of its traditions, yet striving to keep pace with the emerging ideologies around the world. There was immense confidence in the voices that united in song, and an incredible dream in the eyes that followed the flutter of the brand new flag all over the country. It was 15 August 1947. And a civilisation four thousand years old was witnessing the birth of a nation.

The birth had not been painless. There had been decades of revolt and struggle for freedom, bloodshed and betrayal, meticulous negotiations with the British rulers. Finally, the country had been chopped up, and its people torn away from their homes to carve out another nation from the flesh of India: Pakistan. And after the cries had died down and the last train had left for Pakistan, tightly shuttered and trailing blood, India was ready to face its future as a new nation, alive with an enormous hope that shone through its tears. It had a tryst with destiny, as the country's first prime minister, Jawaharlal Nehru, had said, and it was ready.

Thus, India, the peninsula bordered by China and Nepal in the north, Burma in the east and the Indian Ocean in the south, came to be bordered, apart from Afghanistan, by Pakistan in the west. It had a pocket in the east that was East Pakistan then and is now Bangladesh. It remains vast, though sliced up, and stretches from the cool silvery fringes of the Himalaya in the north to the turquoise spread of the Indian Ocean in the south. The western and eastern shores of the giant peninsula are washed by the Arabian Sea and the Bay of Bengal. Bang in the centre of the southern peninsula is the Deccan plateau, and the Thar desert nestles in the northwest. The rest of the country, barring the hills of the northeast, is mostly a long, green stretch of soft plains, watered by rivers like the Ganga and Yamuna in the north, and Kaveri and Godavari in the south. It is a country crafted out of nature's beauty and the dreams of an ancient, pluralist society. For like the variety in its topography, there is an amazing variety in the country's people and cultures, in its ideologies and beliefs, in its heritage and evolving realities.

It is a country primarily rooted in Hindu philosophy, where the majority is still Hindu. But it is also a country that has been under Muslim rule through the ages, where Muslims constitute a minority of about one hundred million, roughly the same as their number in Pakistan. It has a significant population of Buddhists, Sikhs, Jains, Zoroastrians and Jews, and has had Christians since almost the inception of Christianity. It prides itself on being the

A 'patriotic' sadhu with pictures of gods, a pair of cymbals and the national flag at the Kumbha Mela.

A giant statue of the Jain saint, Mahavira—a modern masterpiece, located near the Qutb Minar, New Delhi.

The presence of the Hindu priest is essential for conducting prayers and religious ceremonies and rituals. In villages and smaller towns, the priest continues to wield considerable power.

birthplace of two major world religions: Hinduism and Buddhism. And it is the world's largest democracy.

Above all, it is built on the ideals of equality, liberty and fraternity, where all are equal in the eyes of the law and every individual, irrespective of religion, caste or gender, has the same set of rights by the constitution. There are lapses—women are harassed for dowry, inter-caste marriages are opposed, there are spurts of communal violence. But no law, except perhaps the jungle's, can boast the absence of crime. And it is important to realise that the violence and injustice that India keeps crying out against are so clearly embedded in memory precisely because these are unfortunate, sometimes gruesome, aberrations and certainly not the rule. And although the firm belief in communal harmony has had reason to waver recently, secularism is far from losing out to religious fundamentalism.

Although it is true that India has been the birthplace of quite a few religions—Hinduism, Buddhism, Jainism, Sikhism, to name the better known ones—it has never really been a country obsessed with religion. Contrary to popular belief, especially that of the West, India is not a country of mysticism and rope tricks. There is more to the subcontinent than the scriptures and temple inscriptions, and there

A Buddhist monk praying in a monastery in Sarnath, a tiny hamlet near Banaras where Buddha preached his first sermon called 'Turning of the wheel'—the essence of Buddhist teaching.

certainly has never been much space for the likes of Mahesh Yogi. It is a country woven out of divergent trends, diverse realities, various races and a spectrum of intellectual lines of thought. It is the birthplace of the decimal system, of the game of chess and other intensely intellectual, yet non-religious artefacts that the whole world uses today. It is also the country where the art of love-making was perfected, as is evident from the temple sculptures of Khajuraho, or the ancient treatise on the subject, Vatsyayana's *Kamasutra*.

Not surprisingly, the concept of India as the land of magic and mysticism is relatively new. There had always been stories about strange ways of a strange country, mostly passed on by wonder-struck visitors from England during the British Raj. Stories that

A sevadar in the sarovar *surrounding the Harimandir of the Golden Temple, Amritsar, is seen clearing the pool of flotsam—flower petals, leaves, twigs—which keep falling or are blown into the water.*

had led to the Father of the Nation, Mahatma Gandhi, being dubbed a 'naked fakir' by the West. But before the flower children sought nirvana in the heady fumes of a strange Indian philosophy-without-tears, before ethnic chic became fashionable and Hinduism and Buddhism gained a curious cult following in the West, India was not as sweepingly labelled as a magical mystery tour as it is now. Very recently, Western academics have been reminded of Voltaire's belief that the West owed a lot to India, and not exactly in the delectable area of mumbo-jumbo. The gifts were in sharp focus: 'our numbers, our backgammon, our chess, our first principles of geometry, and the fables which have become our own'. Today, that memory seems to have vanished. And somewhere between then and now, India has become a deep, dark world of religious perplexities, incomprehensible superstitions and good old magic.

It is a country where almost a billion people share 3,287,263 square kilometres between them. Of this, almost 75 per cent live in rural areas. A little more than 52 per cent are literate, and female literacy is at 40 per cent. Several languages and cultures have flourished in the different regions of this subcontinent, the diversity lending a sparkling variety to its rich texture. There are 32 states and union territories, and the country balances a union government at the centre with the federal system by a careful distribution of responsibilities. There are over 700 languages and dialects. In fact, the 1961 census specified 1,652, a figure that was rapidly revised thereafter. Only 18 languages are officially recognised. Curiously, however, the government-run organisation for literary activities, the Sahitya Akademi, gives away awards in 22 languages. So much for official figures.

But India has never been a stickler for official norms. Society is based as much on traditional codes of behaviour as on written laws. Most of its heritage comes from the oral tradition. Even today, systems of alternative medicine, classical dance and music depend more on the teacher-pupil 'lineage' and particular school of learning than on official texts. It is probably this ability to grasp a situation in its totality, this extra-textual wisdom that helps the country where 48 per

A view of the Prayag ghat as seen from the Ganges river. The ghats of Banaras stretch for five kilometres along the winding river front. Some, many centuries old, are known by the names of the donors—Scindia ghat, Bhonsale ghat.

cent are illiterate to form not just the world's largest democracy, but an amazingly mature one at that.

The people of India may be largely uneducated, poor and tradition-bound, but they have shown a remarkable ability to voice their opinions and be heard. They have repeatedly thrown out the ruling party and ushered in a new government. And sacked the new lot as well, at the next hustings, if they failed to deliver. Maybe that does not lend an enviable political stability to the nation, maybe that affects the economy, but it does keep the leaders of the enormous nation on their toes. And by exercising their franchise, the billions in India gain what the lack of literacy, high infant mortality rates and looming poverty line threaten to take away: a sense of power, self-respect and the dignity that comes with it.

India is too vast, too fascinating and too diverse a country to be gathered into an easy book. There are several layers to it, and trying to discover the true India beneath the various strata would be like peeling away at an onion. The layers that baffle and amaze, the clash of ideas and beliefs, the conflicting images which seem to play with one's sanity are not films that veil the land. They are the land. And together, they make up the network of realities that is India.

2
Flashback

There is no reason to suspect that the bewildering diversity that India offers sprung up out of nowhere. The process got some help through the centuries from various invaders who trooped into the country, customs and all, and mingled with the locals. Today, after four thousand years of racial, cultural and religious intermingling, one can hardly fish out the true-blue native Indian.

The visits probably started with the Aryans, the nomads from Central Asia who made their way through the mountain passes of the northwest and settled down in northern India around 2000 BC. Their advent ended one of the world's earliest and most sophisticated civilisations, which had flourished in the Indus river valley for at least a thousand years.

Excavations at Mohenjodaro and Harappa (both in what is now Pakistan) and later at Lothal, Gujarat, revealed clues to an advanced society. The Indus Valley people had careful town planning, well-developed engineering skills and a sophisticated sense of community hygiene—as evident from the covered central drainage system and organised garbage collection in their towns. They lived in houses made of burnt bricks, used clay pots and urns much like those still used in Indian villages, decorated their homes with paintings and sculpture and gave their children a range of toys fashioned out of clay. They even had priests to save their souls. And although the Indus script has not yet been deciphered fully, it is clear that in sophistication this civilisation rivalled those in Sumeria and Egypt.

An Odissi dancer performs at the Sun Temple in Konarak, Orissa, built in the 13th century, in the form of an immense chariot. A class by itself, the temple is largely in ruins; yet the scale of its conception and execution is awesome.

But then the Aryans arrived, and an urban civilisation gave way to a pastoral lifestyle. But with them came the first anchor of Indian philosophy: the Vedas. Composed sometime between 1500 and 1200 BC, these collections of hymns probe the meaning of life and nature. Apart from being the well-spring of Hindu religion, these are also the root of traditional Indian music and dance, of poetry and theatre, of medicine and the sciences. The four Vedas—Rig, Sama, Yajur and Atharva—were poetic portrayals of man's quest for knowledge. A quest which continued through the oral tradition, through the *Ramayana* and *Mahabharata*, and was crystallised in the philosophical treatises of the Upanishads around 550 BC. Today, unfortunately, one seems to forget that Hinduism is not a religion. It is a philosophy that was later codified into an organised religion, to be exploited through the centuries by power-mongers who saw a political arsenal in rite and ritual.

With the growth of agriculture came complex societies. And simple norms of behaviour, evolved for the smooth running of the social machinery, hardened into inscrutable codes of conduct. And nowhere was the tyranny of religion more pronounced than in the caste system. This began as a job-oriented stratification of society where the four castes were held together by mutual interdependence. The Brahmins dealt with the scriptures and learning, the Kshatriyas were the politicians ruling the kingdom, the Vaishyas kept the economy going and the Sudras provided the manual labour. And although philosophers were not exactly kings, as in Plato's stratification, Brahmins, the men of learning, occupied the top slot.

Later, with the growing importance of commerce and politics, the Brahmins were hard put to retain their supremacy. Besides, by the sixth century BC, the polarisation between the privileged and the deprived was enormous. And Hinduism met its first challenge—from a fledgling faith that slowly spread its roots all over the country and later across the world: Buddhism.

Gautama Buddha was a young prince from the foothills of the Himalaya. And one night in 540 BC, he walked out of his palace into the silence of the unknown, seeking truth. When he found it, he became the Buddha, the Enlightened One. And he turned a peripatetic teacher. There is suffering in this world, he taught, which is caused by desire, and by removing desire one can put an end to suffering and attain nirvana or enlightenment. Against the large pantheon of gods and goddesses in Hinduism, there was no god in Buddhism, no idol worship, no rite or ritual. It was a private search for detachment from worldly desire, a search for compassion and peace.

A few years before the Buddha, another seeker had left his princely home on another spiritual quest. And the findings of Mahavira were remarkably similar to those of the Buddha. Only, Mahavira's religion was named Jainism. And he was not the founder, but twenty-fourth in the long line of 'pathfinders' or Tirthankaras. Like Buddhism, Jainism emphasised non-violence and renunciation, and also sought enlightenment. However, although Jainism flourished in India, it did not quite enjoy the phenomenal success of Buddhism. This may have had something to do with royal patronage. Three centuries after the Buddha, a certain emperor stood in a battlefield in Orissa, trying to feel victorious as he surveyed the lifeless bodies strewn around him. Or so the story goes. For once, the invincible Maurya emperor, Ashoka, did not see the bulging boundaries of his empire, he saw the enormous suffering it had brought about. Following an instant change of heart, he embraced Buddhism and dedicated his life—not to mention his considerable political clout— to spreading the religion. Inscribed pillars came up all over the land praising the Buddha. The message of Dhamma or the Buddhist faith were carved out on rocks and stupas (the Buddhist reliquaries). And monasteries dotted his magnificent empire—the largest in India till the British built theirs. He sent his close family members as emissaries to other lands, including Sri Lanka and the Far East, where Buddhism still flourishes.

Meanwhile, Darius I of Persia had annexed the northwest. Later, in 326 BC, Alexander arrived, remarked on the wonder that was India and conquered another chunk of the north. A remarkable change in the culture of the region followed, most clearly seen in the arts. Ancient Greek forms and lines merged with Buddhist spirituality to give birth to Gandhara art. Around that time, India produced a remarkable ruler, Chandragupta Maurya, and his Brahmin minister, Chanakya. Writing under the pen-name of Kautilya, this mentor of Chandragupta produced India's first political treatise, the *Arthashastra*, laying down the rules of governance and economy in shrewd detail—much like Machiavelli did, centuries later.

Dating back to 200 BC, the cave paintings of Ajanta in Maharashtra portray life in the light of Buddhism. Nearby are the Ellora caves, noted for their magnificent sculptures depicting scenes from all faiths of the era: Buddhism, Jainism and Hinduism.

By AD 40 the Scythians or Sakas had conquered parts of western India. In AD 78, they codified the Indian calender that is still in use, and the Saka era began. Indian art and culture got a shot in the arm with the Guptas (AD 319 to AD 606). This was the time of India's literary renaissance, when poets like Kalidasa graced King Vikramaditya's court and added a richer texture to the flourishing empire, which had by now spanned the whole of northern India and parts of the Deccan. Art reached a new high, as evident from the cave paintings of Ajanta and Ellora and the architecture of Sanchi and Sarnath. This was the Golden Age. And it gave birth to classics like Kalidasa's *Abhijnana Shakuntalam*, a sensitive tale of love, betrayal and the larger truth of the human condition.

This was also the time of Hindu revivalism. Buddhism and Jainism were on the decline. Incidentally, south India was never directly affected by the goings-on in the north. Shielded from the rest of the country by the Vindhya mountain range, and from the rest of the world by the oceans framing it, the southern peninsula developed its own identity. But the seas had opened up enormous possibilities of international business relations. Trade with Egypt and Rome gave way to trade with other countries of Southeast Asia, and the flourishing economy through centuries saw artistic representation in the temples and monasteries of southern India. With trade came the exchange of cultural values, of religion and myth. Buddhism as well as Hinduism crossed the seas. And today there are more Buddhists in Southeast Asia, and probably more versions of the *Ramayana* in Indonesia and Thailand than in the country of their birth.

A lot of the credit for this export of culture goes to the aggressive marketing tactics of the southern kings—the Cholas, Pandyas, Chalukyas and Pallavas—who carried Indian culture to Sri Lanka, China, Thailand, Indonesia, Cambodia and Malaysia. Their passion for beauty lives on in hundreds of monuments in India, or in little corners of foreign lands like the exquisite Buddhist stupa of Angkor Vat in Cambodia.

The sculptures on the seashore of Mahabalipuram, in Tamil Nadu, were carved between 600 and 700 AD. Arjuna's Penance, *a relief work on a rock surface, depicts the Pandava prince, Arjuna, in meditation, hoping for a boon from Lord Shiva.*

Art flourished under the ninth century Chola kings, whose patronage of architecture on the scale of the Thanjavur temple is legendary. Besides, they conquered almost all of the Deccan before reaching out beyond the seas. And fired by the desire to push the boundaries of his kingdom to the revered Ganga, the eleventh century emperor Rajaraja Chola fought his way up from the deep south and reached the holy river. He took back the sacred water and mixed it with the waters of the Kaveri, since then known as the Ganga of the south. A whole new city was set up to mark this occasion, named Gangaikondacholapuram, 'the city of the Chola conqueror of the Ganga'. His son, Rajendra Chola, expanded their empire to Sri Lanka, the Maldives and Indonesia. His kingdom across the seas did not last long. But the traditions, cultural values, epics and religion that went with his sceptre still survive.

In the meantime, Muslims swept into the country up north. They came through the northwest, and though there were several brave kings among the Rajputs of west India—the Kshatriyas or warrior castes—since they were perennially fighting among themselves, they could offer no resistance to the Turks. Of the Muslim invaders, Mahmud of Ghazni was the first to make a lasting impact, a thoroughly negative one. He selectively targeted the rich temples of north India. The Iconoclast, they called him, the Idol-breaker. But then, these were raids for petty wealth, not for political power. The rule of the sword and the Koran began with the advent of Mohammed Ghori in 1192. But Ghori had no son to bear his standard and when someone lamented the fact, he is believed to have said, 'Have I not thousands of children in my Turkish slaves?' Sure enough, after Ghori's death in 1206, his slave, Qutb-ud-din Aibak, became the first Sultan of Delhi and started what is rather bluntly known as the Slave Dynasty. A staunch Muslim trying to establish Islam in what he probably believed to be a pagan country, he plundered temples and used the material to build mosques. And having collected a lot of red sandstone and white marble at one point, he began building a minaret. The Qutb Minar, at 250

The Qutb Minar in Delhi, the tallest minaret in the world, built in the thirteenth century, is a symbol of Islamic grandeur.

feet, is the tallest minaret in the world.

Qutb-ud-din was succeeded by his trusted slave, Iltutmish, who carried on the expansion and following the invasion of the Mongols in 1221, led by the infamous Genghis Khan, made Muslim power a force to reckon with in the country. Strangely enough, this devout Muslim passed over his sons and chose his daughter as his successor. But Raziya Sultana, the only Muslim woman ever to rule India, found her courage and sincerity no match for the religious convictions of her ministers. And going by the Prophet's words that 'the people that makes a woman its ruler will not find salvation', they chose salvation over political stability. The young Sultana, who had given up her veil and led her troops fearlessly into battle, was tricked and killed in 1240, after three years in power. A period of turmoil followed until a slave of Iltutmish, who had served Raziya, and her successors as well, took control. Balban was more of a king than a blue blood prince could ever be. He had ruled for 40 years, as minister and as sultan, and had played the severe monarch who never laughs. His empire stretched from Bengal to Sind. After his death, the Khaljis took over.

Ala-ud-din Khalji was a relentless conqueror and a shrewd politician. Having usurped the throne after murdering his learned and benevolent uncle, the illiterate but valiant Ala-ud-din expanded the Delhi Sultanate into the Deccan by a judicious mix of bravery, treachery and outright lying. He left behind a trail of blood and some splendid creations of architecture. The Siri Fort and the gateway to the Qutb Minar, both in Delhi, stand testimony to the beautiful blending of Turkish and Indian styles as foreign ideas were given shape by local craftsmen.

Architecture flourished even more in the days of the Tughlaqs, who created the city of Tughlaqabad next to Delhi. The most interesting of them was Mohammad bin Tughlaq, a brilliant eccentric born much ahead of his time. Well-versed in Indian and Greek philosophy, Persian poetry and many languages, a scholar of mathematics and the sciences with an exquisite taste for the arts, this visionary brought immense misery upon his people by his hasty implementation of unorthodox ideas. For example, he introduced token currency in copper to replace gold and silver coins, a step in the direction of modern paper money. Unfortunately, in the days before a government mint, counterfeiting copper coins was child's play. And as every household became a factory of copper tokens, his land was flooded with fake currency and his treasury was impoverished.

Babar, founder of the Mughal dynasty, depicted in a miniature painting—a distinct style of art brought to India by the Mughals.

Tughlaq's unpopularity climaxed when he decided to move his capital from Delhi to Daulatabad, 'the abode of wealth', in the Deccan. As his empire was spreading steadily in the south, a central capital made more sense than a distant capital in the north. But the sultan was not thinking of moving his seat of government alone. He planned to move Delhi, bag and baggage. So thousands of unhappy souls set off with their children and elderly on this long march to a strange land 700 miles away, following a king they believed to be clinically insane as he uprooted them from their homes and ancestral lands. Many died on the way, from sheer exhaustion if not from a broken heart. In the end, Tughlaq had to abandon the plan. His people came back. But not many had survived the trauma. And no matter how hard the Sultan tried to get the city on its feet again, Delhi had withered and was ready to die.

It didn't, of course. Like the rest of India and its people, Delhi had an uncanny resilience. Two great kingdoms had emerged in the south, the Muslim Bahmani kingdom and the Hindu kingdom of Vijaynagar, and the sultan's borders retreated north. Then in 1398 came the whirlwind invasion of Timur—the emperor of Samarkand who had satisfied his ambitions in Persia, Mesopotamia and Afghanistan before turning to India. The Sultanate collapsed dutifully.

After a brief intervention by the Afghan Lodhis, the throne of Delhi went to a man descended from two of India's biggest scourges, Timur and Genghis Khan. A prince who ascended the throne of Timur as a child but was later confined to Kabul, a man as well-trained in war as in poetry—a man named Babar.

Curiously, it was an uncle of the last Lodhi king who had ushered Babar into India, begging him to save the land from his nephew's despotism. Not that Babar needed much begging. The Mughals—a name derived from 'Mongol', Babar's ancestral stock on his mother's side—took over the throne in 1526, and ruled for three centuries. The land flourished in every sense, administration was perfected in detail, culture underwent sweeping changes. It saw the birth of India's hallmark of grandeur, the Taj Mahal. But the love of beauty was not limited to magnificent mausoleums. It was evident in the daily lives of the early Mughal emperors. Their palaces were fitted with 'air-conditioners' which came in the shape of fountains and artificial streams. The Mughal gardens, like the Shalimar gardens in Kashmir, in their minutely planned finery with little rivulets running through lush greenery and rocks reflected the splendour that had become synonymous with Mughal culture. Like the timeless favourites that India flaunts even today: Mughal miniature paintings and Mughal cuisine.

Meanwhile Babar defeated the Afghans and the gallant Rajputs with his new

Humayun's tomb, where the Mughal king rests, was built by his wife, Haji Begum. Set amidst formal gardens with huge domes and high arches, it was a predecessor to the Taj Mahal.

import: cannon. But unfortunately, it is not for the introduction of gunpowder or for founding a magnificent empire that Babar is most remembered in today's India. He stalks Indian politics for a less significant feat of his: a mosque that he built in Ayodhya, Uttar Pradesh.

Legend marks this as the birthplace of Ram, mythical hero of the *Ramayana*. Some claim that the mosque, known as the Babri Masjid, was built following the destruction of a temple that stood on the sacred spot. This sixteenth century mosque was demolished by Hindu fanatics in December 1992. This sparked off a rash of riots, and marked the darkest phase in secular India's history. However, back in the 1520s, Babar probably did not know that his act as a Muslim imperialist would trigger a reaction more than 450 years later. He had died within four years of his arrival in India, leaving the business of consolidating his empire to his son, Humayun, who was rather unsuccessful at the task. Although lovingly named 'Humayun' or 'the fortunate', this monarch seemed to personify misfortune. His brothers knifed him in the back, his kingdom broke out in rebellion and the mightiest Afghan ruler, Sher Shah, usurped his throne. An astute strategist, Sher

Shah's most remarkable feat was the building of the Grand Trunk Road that connected Punjab with Bengal, and which ran across the expanse of his empire. Till his death, this ruler with enormous military talent and administrative wisdom kept his rapidly expanding empire in tight control. Law and order peaked and even petty theft, let alone armed rebellion, was practically unheard of.

Meanwhile, Humayun was in the wilderness. For 15 years the king without a kingdom wandered about, sustained by his love of learning, belief in tolerance and sense of justice. And finally, six months after he regained his throne in 1555— a decade after Sher Shah was killed in battle—he slipped on the stairs of his library and fell to his death.

Humayun's 13-year-old son, Akbar, born in exile, took over. Akbar proved to be one of the greatest emperors ever to rule India. Unlike previous Muslim rulers, Akbar realised the folly of trying to subjugate the Hindus in Hindustan, and concentrated on winning them over by benevolence and trust. He ensured the loyalty of some Hindu royal families by marrying their princesses. He had a host of Hindu advisors and administrators. He abolished the *jizya*, a tax on Hindus that the Muslim rulers had introduced.

Triggered by his deep interest in religious speculation, Akbar started dialogues between all religions, where Muslims, Hindus, Jains, Zoroastrians, Jews and Christians thrashed out their differences. In the end he formed his own syncretic faith, the 'Din-i-Ilahi' or 'the religion of God', a synthesis of various religious ideas based on a mystical liberalism. In this he was considerably influenced by both Muslim and Hindu mysticism—Sufism and the Bhakti cult. Yet, in his last moments, curious stalwarts of all faiths crowded around Akbar's deathbed trying to figure out whose god the emperor would say his final prayers to. It seems the exercise was inconclusive, and everyone went back feeling cheated.

Not surprisingly, orthodox Muslims had cringed as the young monarch introduced Hindu festivals in his court, took up the Rajasthani turban and flaunted the *tilak*—a Hindu ceremonial mark made by vermilion or sandalwood on the forehead. His many marriages to Hindu princesses, especially the powerful Rajput princesses, had already established a Hindu cultural presence in his harem of 300 wives. His son Jehangir was born of a Rajput princess and went on to marry many such princesses himself. Clearly, the Prophet had lost out to *realpolitik*. This process of integration through religion and culture paid off brilliantly. The masses were relieved, and the bravest warriors, the Rajputs, who had through the centuries shown a marked preference for death over dishonour and thus seemed biologically incapable of betrayal, became Akbar's trusted allies.

As his empire grew, so did the arts. Akbar employed scholars to translate important texts from all languages and religions into Persian, and created a new library where Turkish chronicles, Sanskrit classics and Latin gospels were given equal respect. Well, almost. There were cases like that of Badauni, the court translator and secret chronicler of Akbar's life and times, labouring with the *Mahabharata*. Having decided that the Hindu epic was a bunch of 'puerile absurdities' he had sadly accepted the inevitable: 'But such is my fate, to be employed on such works!' In the visual arts, the emperor had set up a posse of Hindu and Persian illustrators who created the beautiful mix of Persian and Hindustani traditions that is the hallmark of Mughal painting. He had brought the revered Tansen to his court as the master of music. Legend has it that by his perfect rendition of the various *ragas*, Tansen could wring a monsoon shower from a cloudless sky, or spark off a blazing fire out of nowhere. The emperor also set new standards of splendour in architecture.

As a ruler, Akbar introduced many social reforms, not all of which were successful. His attempts at standardising the weights and measures of the land, and pushing for a liberal education for children were more effective than his efforts at abolishing child marriage and *sati*—tangles that were left for the British to solve a couple of centuries later, and which still crop up occasionally to embarrass twentieth-century India.

Akbar's son, Jehangir, was more interested in aesthetics than in conquests, partly because he inherited a vast and stable empire. Everything from birds to terminally ill people were diligently sketched, and European paintings copied to perfection.

He fell in love with a Persian widow of 34, later known as Nurjahan or 'the light of the world'. Clearly middle-aged if not elderly by Mughal standards, Nurjahan,

An aerial view of the entrance of Akbar's tomb at Sikandra, ten kilometres from Agra.

with grown children from her first marriage, was an unlikely candidate for empress, especially since there was a harem full of nubile young beauties from across the country. But the emperor's favourite queen, famed for her beauty and skills in poetry, the arts and hunting, soon became the surrogate ruler, as Jehangir went after the mysteries of nature. And Nurjahan's niece, Mumtaz Mahal, was to marry Jehangir's son and heir, Shah Jehan, whose devotion to her inspired the most exquisite memorial to love, the Taj Mahal.

Shah Jehan was considerably influenced by his eldest son, a religious eclectic. Dara Shikhoh, a great sympathiser of Hinduism, was a scholar of the Hindu scriptures and had even translated the Upanishads into Persian. And it was this obvious deviation from Islam of the heir apparent, coupled with the leniency of Shah Jehan, that triggered the fire of rebellion in the power-hungry Aurangzeb, the emperor's third son.

By a clever mix of manipulation and firepower, Aurangzeb wrested the throne from Shah Jehan. He then imprisoned his father, who died eight years later in

Fatehpur Sikri, near Agra—an aerial view of Akbar's capital city for fifteen years, built as a thanksgiving for the birth of heirs to the throne of Hindustan. Situated on a hill, it was abandoned because of lack of water.

solitary confinement. Not even allowed writing paper, the old emperor whiled away his last years staring out of his window towards the sparkling marble domes of the Taj under which his beloved wife had been laid to rest. He may not have known that he would soon be buried beside her. Shah Jehan had dreamed of being buried across the Yamuna in a replica of the Taj made out of black marble, which would face his wife's mausoleum and be connected with it by a bridge. The two identical yet complementary memorials of grandeur would gaze at each other, over the silvery waters of the Yamuna, locked in eternal love. But the dream died with him. Or maybe earlier. For Shah Jehan had witnessed too much to have illusions of grandeur. He had seen the murder of his sons and grandsons by Aurangzeb. And he had been sent the severed head of his favourite son, Dara Shikoh, on a platter.

Clearly more interested in building an empire than building monuments of beauty, Aurangzeb became the last great emperor of India. But what he had gained in territory he had lost in faith. An orthodox Muslim, he systematically undid the closely knit fabric of communal trust that generations of Mughal rule had created. He reimposed the *jizya* tax on Hindus that Akbar had abolished, and destroyed temples to build mosques in their place. Many of these still stand in various parts of India, a bewildering mix of ornate Hindu foundations suddenly lost in a spare Islamic superstr-ucture. The arts and literature plunged to an all-time low; music was banished and in the 50 years that he ruled with an iron hand, this fanatical emperor shattered the image of the Mughals as patrons of culture. Aurangzeb's empire crumbled following his death in 1707. And the dignity of the great Mughals was snuffed out with Nadir Shah's invasion in 1738. The Turk defeated the ruling Mughal, looted Delhi, massacred the people, and having taken the petrified monarch prisoner, departed with most of the legendary riches of the Mughal treasury. This was when India lost Shah Jehan's priceless Peacock Throne, as well as the Kohinoor—the 'mountain of light'—an enormous diamond passed down through generations of Indian kings.

Centuries earlier, the Kohinoor had been presented to the young Humayun by the royal family of Gwalior. When Humayun offered it to his father, Babar, the latter had apparently taken a good look at the diamond, calculated that it would provide for two and a half days of food for the entire world and tossed it back to his son. Legend has it that when Humayun fell seriously ill, Babar had been advised by religious men to offer god his most prized possession in exchange for his son's life. But Babar failed to see the Kohinoor as his most prized possession (probably since the jewel did not belong to him anyway) and offered god his own life instead. Miraculously, the son recovered as Babar went down with fever and died of it.

Right: *Mumtaz Mahal, born Arjumand Banu, met, fell in love with and married Shah Jehan. She died in childbirth after bearing him fourteen children, of which only seven survived.*

Far right: *Shah Jehan, the Grand Mughal, had a passion for architecture. He is best known for building the pristine and magnificent Taj Mahal, in the memory of his wife, Mumtaz Mahal.*

Facing page: *The Taj Mahal, a mausoleum in pure white marble, built by Shah Jehan, is an engineering and architectural masterpiece. Surrounded by gardens and fountains, and flanked by the Jamuna river on one side, it attracts thousands of visitors from all over the world.*

The Kohinoor had then travelled far and wide, as gift or loot. From Agra to Persia to the Deccan and back to the Mughal treasury of Shah Jehan, where it had remained till Nadir Shah's arrival. Of course, it came back to India later, having passed through the hands of the Kabul royals, and found a home in the treasure troves of the Punjab kings, till Punjab was annexed by the British in 1849 and Sir John Lawrence slipped it into his pocket and forgot about it. The 'mountain of light' lay there in relative indignity for a month and a half, after which the Englishman, rather surprised by the enormous jewel on his person, sent it to Queen Victoria. The Kohinoor has been in the Tower of London ever since.

But Sir John Lawrence's disinterest in royal treasures was clearly not representative of the British psyche. It was the lure of India's wealth that had drawn them, like other invaders, to this land. And it is surprising that even after centuries of looting by Persians, Turks, Mongols and others, India still had so much to lose to them. They came as traders, after Queen Elizabeth I granted a monopolistic charter to the East India Company in 1600. And when Emperor Jehangir agreed to a trading arrangement with the fledgling British company, mostly to curb the influence of the Portuguese who had taken over the seas, he could not have dreamt of the consequences.

But there were other powers fighting for control as well. The Rajputs had been a force to reckon with, whether fighting for or against the Mughals. Then came the Marathas who rose to legendary heights under the gallant Shivaji. A tribal chieftain, this clever and brave warrior proved that one did not have to be a Muslim or a high caste Hindu to build a nation. He set up a well-oiled administration and promoted the arts. And his many heroics made him a legend in his lifetime. The southern power continued to grow under the Peshwas who steadily pushed the boundaries of the Maratha empire into Mughal territory. They were finally overpowered by the British in 1803.

Who were the next empire-builders? Like the Mughals, the British steadily extended their control over the land whose hot and humid tropical climate seemed the major enemy, but unlike the Mughals, they had no intention of making this their home. India remained a land of loot, and although British rule ushered in the industrial revolution and brought about many remarkable changes beneficial for India, all that was done more for a smoother functioning of the colonial powers than for the betterment of the people. The land's resources were drained, its people employed to build the economy of the empire across the seas and the country, famed for its splendour, wrung dry.

But in the process, the British succeeded in doing what no ruler, foreign or native, could do before: they finally integrated the patchwork of kingdoms and provinces under a single rule, connected the immense expanse of the empire by a network of railways and telegraph wires, and moulded a pan-Indian conscious-ness out of the scattered provincial identities. And for the first time in the country's history the religious identity of the people had no relevance to the rulers.

The British may have been the only Europeans to build an empire in India, but they were certainly not the only ones who tried. The first to arrive were the Portuguese, led by Vasco da Gama, who sailed around the Cape of Good Hope of Africa and reached India in 1498, much before the first Mughal arrived and more than a century before the East India Company was set up. They were also the last to leave, in 1961. Then there were the British, the Dutch and the French, each trying to gain control and spiking the chances of the others. Like the Portuguese in Goa, the French had taken control of Pondicherry in 1672. And like the Portuguese, they left after the British Raj had moved out.

The British had to clear a lot of ground before they could lay claim to the land.

The eighteenth century saw them waging several wars against the sultans of Mysore, Hyder Ali and his son Tipu Sultan. After Tipu had been killed in 1799, the British turned on the Marathas. Finally there was the Punjab, which after two Sikh wars, buckled under in 1849. The empire had taken shape. It soon stretched from the Indus in the west to Burma in the east, and from the Himalaya in the north to Kanyakumari in the southern tip of the peninsula. It would stay that way for almost a century. But before that the rulers had shifted ground. The sepoys had revolted in 1857 and caused much damage to the empire-building efforts of the British. The mutiny in the ranks had spread to the masses and become a revolt against British rule. It was a minor rumour at first, claiming that the shells the sepoys had to skin with their teeth were greased with pig-fat. Or maybe cow-fat. And between the two options it had defiled almost the entire span of Indian battalions. Muslims regard

Chittorgarh— symbol of Rajput valour and home to Princess Padmini whose legendary beauty lured Alauddin Khalji to a fierce and bloody battle.

pigs to be dirty and Hindus hold cows to be sacred. But however divergent the reasons may be, the result was the same: it was a sin for both. So, convinced that the heathens were bent on packing them off to hell, the Bengal Army lashed out at the foreign rulers. Bengal was the seat of power, and Calcutta the capital of the British Raj. Soon the revolt spread across all of northern India. But it was a sudden revolt, which ended just as abruptly. The Indian soldiers had shaken the elderly monarch, Bahadur Shah Zafar, out of his deep political slumber and proclaimed him their emperor. The last Mughal, in turn, had hastily looked up from his volumes of poetry and dutifully invited the Hindus and Muslims of India to unite and 'end the tyranny and oppression of the infidel and treacherous English'. The words would echo through India for almost another century, as several leaders of the freedom struggle breathed new passion into the same dream. But the British were there to stay. And after a macabre dance of death, the mutiny was over.

However, the revolt had made one thing clear, that to control India, the British would need the power of the crown. Till then, they were functioning under the rather unglamorous title of 'Servant of the East India Company'. So after 250 years of its presence in India, the East India Company was wound up and the British government officially took control. And the last Mughal monarch was packed off to Burma, where he died in bondage. So British rule raged on. Enriching the country with English education, a network of railways and democratic systems of government, yet squeezing the lifeblood out of the masses by its unabated hunger for wealth. Cash crops important for trade, like indigo, eased out food crops. And crazed by hunger and the oppressive rule of a racist regime, the fantasy of driving the British out gained momentum. In the meantime, an Indian identity was steadily emerging from the ashes of regional fiefdoms. The newly educated strata, buzzing with ideas of liberty, equality and fraternity popularised by the French Revolution of 1789, were ready to carve out a long-term plan of ridding themselves of the colonial power. And the fight against the British slowly snowballed into a national movement.

The Indian National Congress, set up in 1885 by a band of intellectuals with a passion for politics, demanded a representative government and a degree of self-rule. And as the political influence of the educated class emerged stronger than ever, the British decided to break up Bengal, the seat of this steady rise of the intellegentsia. In 1905, it was split into East Bengal and West Bengal, a partition that would have a devastating effect on the Indian nation four decades later. The act unleashed an enormous wave of nationalism where Hindus and Muslims joined forces to protest the split. Spearheaded by intellectuals like Rabindranath Tagore, this new surge of patriotism added a cultural angle to the dream of political freedom. And with it the *Swadeshi* movement, advocating the boycott of British goods, soared to incredible heights.

Unfortunately, as the *Swadeshi* movement intensified, leaders began to fall out with each other. Revolutionaries like Bal Gangadhar Tilak, Bipin Chandra Pal, Aurobindo Ghosh and Lala Lajpat Rai pressed for immediate grabbing of power through a full-blooded rebellion, whereas the moderates in the Congress like Gopal Krishna Gokhale, Surendranath Banerjee and Madan Mohan Malviya held on to the earlier ideal of checking British atrocities and exploitation while avoiding a head-on collision. And though in 1911 the British annulled the partition of Bengal and moved their capital from Calcutta to Delhi, the flames of violence could hardly be checked.

To complicate things further, the First World War was declared. Turkey, a Muslim country, had joined Germany against the Allies, and Indian Muslims grew further alienated from their rulers. And though the British declared in 1919 their intention of charting out a path towards self-governance for Indians, it did not stop the rulers and the ruled from being locked in innumerable clashes. Only the enormous strength of a frail, middle-aged vegetarian in a peasant's *dhoti*, could check the incredible spread of violence in a country charged with a longing for freedom. Mohandas Karamchand Gandhi, a lawyer, was back from South Africa, making a career switch from legal to political justice. As he felt his way around in the struggle for independence, Jalianwalla Bagh burst upon the country. And Gandhi was swept into the frontlines of the freedom movement.

It was a massacre of innocents in Jalianwalla Bagh, Punjab. In April 1919, a British army contingent emptied its guns into an unarmed crowd gathered for a meeting in an enclosed area. Hundreds died in this unprovoked attack. And Gandhi launched his own offensive against the British: a policy of non-violent, passive resistance. The bright young civil servant, Subhas Chandra Bose, gave up his government job; renowned lawyers like Chittaranjan Das and Motilal Nehru hung up their robes.

The movement spread like wildfire, with an increasing number of people from all corners of the country refusing to have anything to do with the British or their goods. It was not just his saintly vision of righteousness that made Gandhi's *Satyagraha*, a search for Truth, a phenomenal success. It was the uncanny knack he had of gauging the emotional needs of the people. For the first time India had a leader with genuine mass appeal who could relate to the intellectuals as well as the farmers. But he believed that one could not take a wrong path to reach a right aim. Therefore, throughout his struggle for freedom, Gandhi would insist on non-violence. Whether it was a march to Dandi, protesting the lopsided salt tax, or the spinning of *khadi* for effective boycott of British textiles, he chose the same weapon: civilised behaviour.

But not everyone was ready to sit back and be killed, an occupational hazard of being Gandhi's follower. Hot-blooded revolutionaries wanted action. Subhas

India Gate, completed in 1931, was built as a memorial to the soldiers who died in the First World War, and the British and Indians who died in the North West Frontier and the Third Afghan War. It also commemorates the Indian soldiers who died during the liberation of Bangladesh in 1971.

Chandra Bose, who had emerged as a powerful leader of the extremists, bared his passionate soul to the masses, promising liberty at a price many were ready to pay: 'Give me your blood, and I will give you freedom.' And hundreds of young dreamers offered theirs. Meanwhile, the Second World War had broken out, creating a political deadlock in India. Seizing his chance, Bose joined forces with the Japanese against the British and formed the Indian National Army. He even inaugurated the 'Government of Free India' safely away from British territory in Singapore. And after repeated attempts at dislodging the colonial power, the young revolutionary left the country. He did not return. Some believe that he died in an aircrash. Some regard that to be yet another British plea to derail the freedom struggle, and assume their hero to be alive, somewhere 'out there'.

In the meantime the Muslim League, formed following the partition of Bengal, had emerged as a major rival of the Hindu-dominated Congress. And although Gandhi's fervent attempts at communal harmony had somehow managed to keep the Muslims in the mainstream of the nationalist movement, under the leadership of Muhammed Ali Jinnah, the League broke away and aired its own set of demands.

It pushed for a separate state for Indian Muslims. The impact of these rumblings of 1937 were finally felt a decade later when the British packed up and left, having first broken up their former empire to form the Muslim state of Pakistan.

Meanwhile, Gandhi launched the Quit India Movement in 1942. 'Leave India to God', he told the rulers. 'If that is too much, then leave her to anarchy.' They did not leave at all. Not till five years later. The Second World War had shattered the myth of European superiority and colonialism was clearly on its way out. Independence for India was just a question of time.

The time arrived on the midnight of 15 August, 1947. It was a moment of joy that crystallised the hopes and dreams of generations. India became an independent nation. Rather, it became two independent nations. And Jinnah took control of Pakistan. The only one deeply unhappy at this moment of victory was the man who had come to be known as the Father of the Nation. For Gandhi, this victory was only partial.

But Pakistan was not born out of an aseptic operation. The partition followed a trail of blood, as Punjab and Bengal went under the knife. For in certain areas people had a choice, between the Islamic nation and the mother country that promised to respect all religions. As thousands of petrified Muslims fled to Pakistan, and Hindus crossed over into India, Gandhi's ideals were drowned in the terrifying surge of communal hysteria.

Then there was the added problem of Kashmir, a Muslim dominated country ruled by a Hindu king who could not decide which way to go. By the time he finally chose the secular country, the harm had been done. And Kashmir has since remained the bone of contention between India and Pakistan.

Five months after independence, on the morning of January 30, 1948, a fanatic fiercely opposed to Gandhi's philosophy of Hindu-Muslim brotherhood touched the feet of the Mahatma, straightened up and pulled the trigger. It was the final proof that Gandhi's truth had crumpled up and died.

Facing page: *On January 26, 1950, India's constitution came into effect. For almost half a century since then, on that day every year, thousands show up to honour the moment. The Republic Day Parade, however, is a well-rehearsed part of the official celebrations.*

जय हिन्द

15TH AUG 1947
12 AS INDIA POSTAGE

Here is a passage in the Atharva Veda in which it is said that when his was raised upwards he found also the oblique sides and all other directions in him...

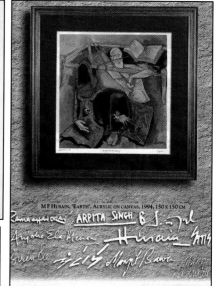

M F HUSAIN, 'EARTH', ACRYLIC ON CANVAS, 1994, 150 x 150 CM

SIGNED FRAMED PRINTS FROM THE BEST
IN CONTEMPORARY INDIAN ART
ART TODAY

TODAY IS THE DAY
OF THE
PREMIERE OF "WOMAN"
NATIONAL STUDIOS' *FIRST & BRILLIANT PICTURE*

The Story written by Mr. BABUBHAI MEHTA, author of many film successes, deals with life, manners and customs in an Indian village and portrays the Indian ideal of womanhood.

AN ALL STAR-CAST

SURENDRA, screen's favourite idol, playing the character part, SARDAR AKHTAR, JYOTI, ARUN, YAKUB, VATSALA, HARISH, KANHIYA-KUMTEKAR, SUNALINI DEVI & LAL, BRIJRANI.

A unique and sensational presentation of Indian village life and culture in its pristine purity.

A drama of human emotions, and stirring conflict between mother and woman, packed with excitement.

A picture which shows the strong current of life pulsating in 7,00,000 villages of India.

A powerful theme powerfully acted.

"WOMAN"
THE PICTURE OF THE YEAR
directed with consummate skill and ability by one of India's leading Director, MAHBOOB.

AT PATHE CINEMA
Daily at 3-30, 6-30 & 9.30 P.M.

GANDHI IS KILLED BY A HINDU;
INDIA SHAKEN, WORLD MOURNS;
15 DIE IN RIOTING IN BOMBAY

THREE SHOTS FIRED
Slayer Is Seized, Beaten After Felling Victim on Way to Prayer

DOMINION IS BEWILDERED

Nehru Appeals to the Nation to Keep Peace—U. S. Consul Assisted in Capture

By ROBERT TRUMBULL
Special to The New York Times

NEW DELHI, India, Jan. 30—Mohandas K. Gandhi was killed by an assassin's bullet today. The assassin was a Hindu who fired three shots from a pistol at a range of three feet.

The 78-year-old Gandhi, who was the one person who held discordant elements together and kept some sort of unity in the turbulent land, was shot down at 5:15 P. M. as he was proceeding through the Birla House gardens to the pergola from which he was to deliver his daily prayer meeting message.

The assassin was immediately seized.

He later identified himself as Nathuram Vinayak Godse, 36, a Hindu of the Mahratta tribes in Poona. This has been a center of resistance to Gandhi's ideology.

Mr. Gandhi died twenty-five minutes later. His death left all India stunned and bewildered at the direction that this newly independent nation would take without its "Mahatma" (Great Teacher).

The loss of Mr. Gandhi brings this country of 300,000,000 abruptly to a crossroads. Mingled with the sadness in this capital tonight was an undercurrent of fear and uncertainty, for now the strongest influence for peace in India that this generation has known is gone.

[Communal riots quickly swept Bombay when news of Mr. Gandhi's death was received. The Associated Press reported that fifteen persons were killed and more than fifty injured before an uneasy peace was estab-

MOHANDAS K. GANDHI
The New York Times

All Britain Honors Gandhi;
Truman Deplores Tragedy

By HERBERT L. MATTHEWS
Special to The New York Times

LONDON, Jan. 30—Mohandas K. Gandhi, in death, has won the unanimous tribute of Britons—something he never hoped for or expected during his life. Nowhere outside of India has the shock of his assassination contained the feelings and emotions evident here today because Britain and Mr. Gandhi have been linked for good or evil over the last forty years.

In a special broadcast to the British people tonight the Prime Minister said:

"The voice which pleaded for peace and brotherhood has been silenced, but I am certain that his spirit will continue to animate his fellow countrymen and will plead for peace and concord."

[President Truman and Secre-

U. S. WARNS CITIZENS IN PALESTINE FIGHT
Consulate General Says They Face Loss of Passports and All Protective Rights

By SAM POPE BREWER
Special to The New York Times

JERUSALEM, Jan. 30—United

3

Back to the Future

So India is an ancient civilisation. Its roots, going back thousands of years, are alive in every aspect of its daily life. That lends the country a certain charm. But it does not signify that history is all that India possesses. The true charm of the country runs beyond the wonder of ancient traditions and the beauty crafted out of frilly blue seas and golden sunshine. It lies in the careful balancing of its heritage with the ever-changing reality of the present. It lies in the rich cultural texture of a densely populated country with over 700 languages and dialects. A country that has shown incredible resilience and strength, and has snatched an identity for itself out of the interplay of conflicting cultures and beliefs, and has woven it into a harmonious tradition that finds expression in its culture.

The cultural heritage of India includes the *Raghuvamsam* and *Meghadutam* of Kalidasa, and the Persian-influenced miniatures of Mughal and Rajput

1. *The first conquest of Mt. Everest on the cover of The Times in 1953.*
2. *Commemorative stamp on India's independence.* 3. *An early 20th century illustration of a folk tale from Bengal.*
4. Inauguration of New Delhi 1931 *and other commemorative stamps.* 5. *A dance performance for a British sahib.*
6. *Rabindranath Tagore's erasures on a manuscript of* The Religion of Man *(c. 1930).* 7. *A fine example of Indian contemporary art.* 8. *A typical turn of the century advertisement.* 9. *Films, the most popular form of entertainment in India.*
10. *An illustration from a folk tale of Bengal.* 11. *Ancient coins of India.* 12. *A Mughal miniature portrait of Emperor Jehangir.* 13. *Report of Gandhi's assassination in the* New York Times. *14. Devika Rani, popular actress of the thirties* 15. *A still from Bobby, a famous blockbuster of the seventies.*

paintings. It glances back at the exquisite artistry of the Ajanta and Ellora cave paintings and Rig-vedic poetry, but it goes much beyond that. Today India throbs with a vibrant culture that has as much of Urdu poet Iqbal's mysticism as Bengali litterateur Tagore's world-view, as much of Hindustani classical music as Carnatic. And with the rise of every new style and idea on the international horizon, there is a new turn in Indian culture as well. Even if ever so slight. Even if almost imperceptible. Like Confucius' river, you never take a dip in the same culture twice. Certainly not in India.

The newest entrant in the stream is cinema, which is over a century old. Right after they came up with the cinematograph, the Lumiere brothers took it on a world tour in an attempt to popularise the technique. And a group of Indian elites fell for it right then, in 1896. By the turn of the century, they were making short films of their own. And the first feature film came up in 1913, with Dadasaheb Phalke's cinematic adaptation of history in *Raja Harishchandra*. The idea of cinema as a powerful medium for the masses was born; today popular cinema often takes on the role of king-maker. M. G. Ramachandran, Jayalalitha and N. T. Rama Rao rose to be chief ministers on the strength of their fan following as cine stars. And several used their enormous mass appeal on celluloid to win a place in the parliament, like Vyjayanthimala Bali, Sunil Dutt, Amitabh Bachchan or Vinod Khanna.

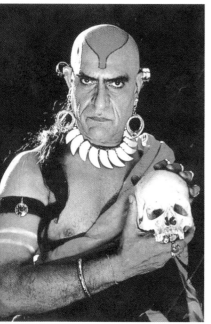 

(Left) Amrish Puri and Amitabh Bachchan, the villain and the hero of the celluloid world, who are immensely popular with the Indian public.

Bachchan, of course, is a living legend. Well over 57, this one-man industry can still carry through a blockbuster on his lanky frame. From a handsome beginning in *Anand* to *Zanjeer*, which yanked him up to the level of a superstar, the 'angry young man' has remained an all-time idol and box-office wonder, greying beard notwith-standing. As has been proved by *Khuda Gawah*, his comeback bid following retirement plans and more recently, by the hit *Bade Miyan Chhote Miyan*. The new breed of stars like Salman Khan, Sanjay Dutt (whose glamour has been somewhat overshadowed by his jail term) Govinda, Akshaye Khanna, Madhuri Dixit, Kajol, among others, lag far behind the grandmaster, their one-dimensional stardom incapable of matching the splendour of Bachchan's enormous presence.

It is hardly surprising that the country that showers so much adulation on celluloid stars also produces the world's largest film footage every year. The medium, born out of the careless indulgence of the British Raj and which grew to be a powerful weapon against the foreign rulers, has covered every social issue from untouchability and child marriage in the silent era, to class struggle and the power of the proletariat in later times. It excelled as a medium of propaganda during the struggle for independence and carried on its struggle after the birth of the nation by lashing out against corruption in the government machinery. It has probed social values and dogmas, raised issues of gender, caste and class. In short, cinema has diligently reflected the changing times and values, and in a country where half the population is still untouched by literacy, it has proved an effective medium of communication that reaches out to the masses.

And though the hub of India's film industry is 'Bollywood', otherwise known as Bombay, the *nouvelle vague* and art film world do not lag far behind. Since Satyajit Ray put Indian cinema on the international map, directors like Ritwik Ghatak, Mrinal Sen, Adoor Gopalakrishnan and Govind Nihalani have lent their own vision to the language of celluloid. Not every art film blossoms into a *Pather Panchali*, but the path carved out by Ray is today well-traversed. So although cinema in India is viewed primarily as the product of 'Bollywood' and its regional counterparts, the legacy of Ray, nurtured by the dreams of Griffith, Eisenstein, Godard, Fellini and Truffaut, cannot be brushed aside.

But social issues and artistic excellence has been balanced for ages in literature. From the novels of Bankim Chandra Chattopadhyay, written in Bengali in the nineteenth century, to the endeavours of the new crop of Indians writing in English, literature has been chronicling society. There have been nationalist concerns in masterpieces like Chattopadhyay's *Anandamath* and Rabindranath Tagore's *Gora*. Or in the poetry of Nazrul Islam. Human relationships in narrower frames have been probed by Sharat Chandra Chatterjee's novels about the Bengali middle class, Premchand's writings on village life. Bibhuti Bhushan Bandyopadhyay's and Tarashankar Bandyopadhyay's portrayals of rural Bengal and tribal life and Phanishwar Nath Renu's works on rural Bihar.

In poetry, there has been a shift from the twelfth century *vachanas* in Kannada and Telugu, through Chandidas' Vaishnavism in Bengali, Kabir's religion of man and Mirabai's love for Krishna in Hindi, to the twentieth century's more sophisticated mysticism of Iqbal and Tagore. There has been pure romance and wonderment at the beauty of nature which, understandably, forms the bulk of modern Indian poetry. Love has mingled with existential *angst* and metaphysical quest, like in the poetry of Jibanananda Das and Amrita Pritam. Through the ages, the 22 literary languages of India (which include English) have produced an excellent body of literature reflecting the times, the values, the concerns, the quests of an ever-changing Indian reality. Unfortunately, due to the lack of an effective link language other than English, and the poverty of translations, most of the country's best writers have remained mere regional stars.

Amitav Ghosh and (left) Salman Rushdie: protagonists of recognised English literary writing of the twentieth century

But those writing in English do not have that handicap. Thus writers like R. K. Narayan, Mulk Raj Anand, Dom Moraes, Nissim Ezekiel and Kamala Das have had a pan-Indian readership, and have been representing contemporary Indian literature in the international arena. They do represent a significant section of the subcontinent's literary work, but it would be a mistake to assume that they make up its basics. And as India becomes increasingly Westernised, the new crop of Indian writers in English become stronger. Following in the footsteps of Salman Rushdie, young authors of the subcontinent have carved out niches for themselves in the Western world. The trend started in the eighties, with new Indian writers sprouting on Western soil. They retained the earthy touch of India, and the exotic stamp that came with it. And the young authors served up ethnic chic from the East through a medium of the West. (Indian English may not exactly be the language of the Queen, but it is English, nevertheless.) And stars were born, like Vikram Seth, the superstar with superbucks, Firdaus Kanga, Allan Sealy, Rohinton Mistry, Amitav Ghosh, Upamanyu Chatterjee, Shashi Tharoor, Amit Chaudhuri, Arundhati Roy and Sunetra Gupta. And many others, mostly with the same winning combination: sparkling, smooth prose, a sensitive eye and a yuppie sense of humour. Unfortunately, unlike the all-time greats of Indian literature, this lot—good but certainly not great—seems to have succumbed to the charms of packaging. And unlike their talented predecessor, most of Rushdie's children lack his sense of history and the playful daring that had cost him his freedom. However, it is thanks to these young authors that the world was shaken out of its suspicion that Indian literature had died with Tagore. And that Rushdie was actually a British masquerading as someone from the subcontinent. Today, the half-caste kids of the Raj have struck back, cutting their way into the international imagination, and making their place among the legal heirs.

Girish Karnad: well-known playwright, film actor and theatre personality; (right) M.F. Husain: internationally acclaimed contemporary artist.

With liberalisation, the growth of the middle class, the rise in literacy and surge in commercialisation, the arts have undergone a sea change of late. There are more sponsors, more consumers and, therefore, more made-to-order art. Which is not to say that 'real' art is dying, or that there is any dearth of talent. There has only been a sharp division between the intellectual and the market-driven art forms, and the latter has soared to immodest heights.

The art that began its journey from the sculptures of 3,000 years ago, that weaved its way through the ancient cave paintings and murals of Ajanta, Hoshangabad, Bhimbhetka, through the mythical stories of Rajput paintings and the vibrant colours of Tanjore, is still alive, and remoulding itself in the patterns of the twentieth century. Gaganendranath Tagore's experiments with lines and paint, Amrita Shergil's forms, Jamini Roy's rekindling of the folk tradition have made way for modern art, ushered in by the Progressive Artists Group of M. F. Husain, Francis Newton Souza, Ara and others. But Husain has progressed far beyond what the fledgling group of artists with fire in their bellies had bargained for. He is not only the best-known artist of the country, but has also managed to bridge the gap between the solemnity of art and the apparent vulgarity of filthy lucre. A master showman, Husain, the barefoot artist, is also one of the richest in the country and keeps the country enthralled by his endless gimmicks and spectacular talent.

Theatre too has undergone a similar change. According to Hindu scriptures, theatre sprouted from the desire of Brahma, the divine father, to entertain the gods. The ritual lost its religious tint ages ago, and today there are more forms of theatre in the folk tradition scattered throughout the country than the picture-frame settings of urban theatre can dream of. Like anywhere else in the world, with the rise of cinema, theatre has been sidelined, and is only frequented by true lovers of the medium. And thanks to talents like Badal Sircar, Habeeb Tanveer, Vijay Tendulkar, B.V. Karanth and Girish Karnad, new theatre in India, whether it is in Marathi,

Bengali, Chhattisgarhi or Kannada, or in any other language of the subcontinent, has come of age.

Like theatre, Indian classical dance too is based on the desire of the gods to be entertained. But unlike theatre, it has retained its ancient form, and although new dialects have emerged, the language remains the same. The main forms of classical dance, Bharatanatyam, Kathakali, Kathak, Manipuri and Odissi, have in common a spectacular rhythm and metaphor. And although new forms have seen various experimentations, the magnificence of the original forms are hard to match.

The classical flavour, however, has not been so rigid in music. With a rich base of classical music—both the northern Hindustani and southern Carnatic—India has graduated to various new trends and styles, drawing on influences from the West and the Far East, from rhythms and tunes across the world. Whether it is vocal music of ghazals, bhajans, kirtans or thumris, or instrumental experiments in the classical and pop traditions, music has been keeping time with the country's heartbeat.

There have been maestros like Ravi Shankar, Ali Akbar Khan, Bade Ghulam Ali, M. S. Subbulakshmi and Amjad Ali Khan in the classical tradition. There have been pop royalty like Rafi, Lata Mangeshkar, Kishore Kumar and Hemanta Mukherjee who have lent their voice to prop up the film industry. And there have been experiments to merge the East with the West. The trend that began when Ravi Shankar matched his sitar to the Beatles' drums and guitars has passed through the hands of experts like Zakir Hussain and L. Subramaniam and has come to rest with the makers of today's pop culture. Curiously, a lot of it seems to be resting with songsters like Baba Sehgal, who keep copying one English number after another, and are sometimes unable to resist the temptation of dressing up like Madonna.

Looking back on the amazing influence of the West on Indian culture today makes one wonder whether the ones who opted out of the identity crisis—of coping with the culture and values one is born in and the lure of international recognition that the West seems to offer—were better off. India has bidden farewell to stars like Hollywood beauty Merle Oberon and rock legend Freddie Mercury, who spent their lives trying to disguise their Indian identity, whose path to stardom necessitated the denial of basic individual truths. Others, like Zubin Mehta and Apache Indian (Steven Kapur) have reached out to touch their roots in the country, however faint they may be today. India, like a mother swelling with pride at her children's success, has claimed a slice of their glory regardless of their own declarations. For it is a country that prides itself upon its people, high or low, and as is the habit with mothers, refuses to let go of a child that has grown apart.

4
The Beauty Myth

After a bird's-eye view of India, it is time for a whistle-stop tour of the country. It is prudent to mention at the onset that finding beauty spots in this land of monks and monkeys is easier for a foreign tourist than an Indian. Indian tourists seem to have an annoying ability to completely miss out the charms of the exotic east. They would, for example, look upon a monkey as a potential thief and not as Lord Hanuman. They wouldn't dream of offering their respects to the holy cow jamming the traffic. They seem to be satisfied only with snow-capped mountains and fun on the beach. Thankfully, India has a choice of both, apart from natural parks, deserts and magnificent monuments.

Delhi

A bewildering mix of tradition and modernity, DELHI, the capital city, can easily jar your senses. Studded with mosques, temples, tombs and monuments of every kind, the centre of the Indian government sums up the adventures that this city has witnessed through the ages. The legendary Pandavas of the *Mahabharata* are said to have ruled from Indraprastha, in the eastern part of the city on the banks of the Yamuna. And the last Hindu kingdom in north India was ruled from an area in south Delhi. Then the Muslims arrived, and from the twelfth century, Delhi was the capital of their Indian empire, till the British took over, shifted the capital to Calcutta (in Bengal), only to return to Delhi in 1911. And though the rulers have

Amidst the quaint charms of Old Delhi, a stone's throw from the Red Fort, lies one of the country's most important mosques, the Jama Masjid. Built in the seventeenth century by Shah Jehan, this memorial to Mughal splendour remains a vibrant centre of worship even today. And on every occasion of special prayer, like Eid, the 300-year-old building comes alive with fresh hopes and dreams.

changed, as have the cars and the skyline, this continues to be the centre of the Indian government.

Old Delhi, the capital of Muslim India, is a maze of narrow lanes. You enter what was once Shahjehanabad, the 'walled city' that Shah Jehan had built in the seventeenth century, and find that the mighty stone wall has crumbled. Ignoring that minor technicality, the city gate stands proud and tall, pretending to control the flow of people. The Red Fort testifies to the exquisite taste of Shah Jehan.

Wrapped in elaborate red sandstone wall, the Lal Qila exemplifies fortified grandeur. The Lahore Gate leads into an arcade, the Meena Bazaar. This was where the ladies of the court came to shop. Pass on to the open courtyard that was once alive with music as the emperor's Nahabat Khana, or gallery for musicians. Walk through the Diwan-i-Am, where the emperor met the general public, and enter the Diwan-i-Khas, where he met VIPs. But the hall you see is not the one that Shah Jehan had created or Aurangzeb had ruled from. That was a tribute to splendour. The lights of chandeliers bounced off the silver ceiling, and in the centre of this shimmering chamber was the Peacock Throne. If there was anything that could rival the Taj Mahal in sheer magnificence, it was this other creation of Shah Jehan's. Guarding the glittering seat of gold stood two exquisite peacocks, crafted out of a mosaic of jewels. This was where the emperor sat. Till Nadir Shah decamped with the throne.

Moti Masjid or the Pearl Masque in the Red Fort, Delhi, is one of Aurangzeb's rare creations of austere beauty.

From the Diwan-i-Khas you move on to the royal baths, sheltered by lofty domes and sporting a fountain in the centre. You walk out and reach the Pearl Mosque. Crafted in marble, this Moti Masjid is one of the few creations of beauty from the reign of Aurangzeb. Finally, you walk out of the Lal Qila and up to the Jama Masjid.

Built by Shah Jehan, this extravagant mosque is the largest in the country and remains an important place of worship. Flanked by majestic gateways, minarets and towers, the Jama Masjid is built out of red sandstone and white marble. And like most monuments in India, whether Hindu or Muslim, it has learnt to balance trade, tourism and faith. Fishmongers, butchers and vegetable vendors breathe new life into the seventeenth century mosque with the crazy buzz of their flourishing bazaar right outside its gates.

You step out of the Jama Masjid and waddle through the sea of traffic, trying not to get run over by buses and horse-driven carts. And having experienced a genial fleecing in the bazaar of Chandni Chowk—where the British had publicly hanged rebels following the Sepoy Mutiny—you reach either a serene Jain temple or the Fatehpuri Masjid, depending on which way the tide of traffic has taken you.

At the northern end of Old Delhi you find the Kashmiri Gate, which saw the crucial fight between the British and the sepoys in 1857. The Mutiny Memorial stands nearby. Beside it looms a tall pillar built by Ashoka, and brought here by Feroze Shah Tughlaq in the fourteenth century. Another Ashokan pillar stands in the Feroze Shah Kotla, near Old Delhi. This was once Ferozabad, the capital of the later Tughlaqs, where, back in January 1399, the mighty Timur kneeled in humility before Allah, taking time off from looting and killing.

A stone's throw from Feroze Shah Kotla is Raj Ghat. Here, on the banks of the sacred Yamuna is a platform of black marble that marks the spot where Mahatma Gandhi was cremated. Since then, dignitaries from around the world have paid their respects to the memory of the Father of the Nation.

Go east and find the Purana Qila or Old Fort, its three imposing gates and broken walls holding up a proud legacy of the Afghan ruler, Sher Shah. Inside the sixteenth century fort is a mosque and a pleasant little octagonal tower made of red sandstone, the Sher Manzil. Humayun, who used this quiet tower as a library, was on his way down from its roof on January 24, 1556, when he heard the summons for evening prayer rise from the mosque. The emperor turned to bow in respect, caught his foot on his robe and tumbled to his death.

Humayun's tomb, just south of the Old Fort, in some ways predicts the Taj Mahal. The high arches and magnificent domes, the beautiful garden, the perfect blending of red, white, yellow and black in the marble and sandstone structure, all point to the making of new concepts in Indian architecture. The grandeur that is born in its graceful lines blossoms fully in the Taj Mahal three generations later.

A short distance away is the Hazrat Nizamuddin, named after the fourteenth century Muslim saint, Nizamuddin Chisti, who is buried here. Legend has it that while Nizamuddin was building this shrine, emperor Ghiyas-ud-din Tughlaq tried taking away Nizamuddin's men for constructing Tughlaqabad. So the holy man cursed the unborn city saying that it would be a ghost town roamed by herdsmen. The curse seems to be still in effect.

The Jantar Mantar in Delhi, an observatory to study the movements of heavenly bodies, was built by Sawai Jai Singh II in 1724.

Near Nizamuddin's shrine is a rather simple tomb of Jahanara, Shah Jehan's daughter. So is there a tomb of one of the greatest Indian poets, Mirza Ghalib who died in 1869: *I lived my life waiting for death to come/ And dead, I still must see what else I face.*

Nearer the centre of the city is India Gate, a memorial to the Indian soldiers. Near it is the President's House, the Rashtrapati Bhavan, a palace set in a sprawling Mughal garden. A stone's throw from this is the Indian seat of power, the Parliament House.

Walking straight down Parliament Street, you may come to a park that houses a startling conglomeration of enormous pink structures. Maharaja Jai Singh II of Jaipur constructed the Jantar Mantar in 1725, to map the course of the sun and planets. And you may not want to miss Hauz Khas, still called a village, which flaunts the best assortment of crumbling edifices in New Delhi. This was Siri, capital of the Khaljis. The Siri Fort nearby, bubbling with intellectual activity, is a lively perch for culture vultures.

Probably the most famous of Delhi monuments is the Qutb Minar, the ornate 73-metre expression of victory of the Afghan kings. Like many monuments, it is made of red sandstone and white marble and was initiated by Qutb-ud-din. Next to it is the first mosque built in India, Qutb-ud-din's Quwwat-ul-Islam Masjid, or the 'power of Islam' mosque.

In the courtyard stands the 7-metre high iron pillar with Sanskrit inscriptions. Dating back to the Gupta period, this structure has perplexed scientists for years with its exceptional ability to stand the ravages of time. Open to the elements for over 2,000 years, the iron pillar shows no signs of rust. And taking a cue from the mysteries of ancient alchemy, it is believed that if you can stand with your back to the pillar and encircle it with your arms, your dreams will come true. So go ahead. Make a wish.

In Taj Territory

Once the capital of India, AGRA is today best known as the city of the Taj Mahal. Built over 21 years (1632-53), and with 20,000 workers, this symbol of Mughal extravagance was created by Shah Jehan as a memorial of love for his wife, Mumtaz

Mahal. The marble monument stands on a raised platform, topped by a huge central dome and four smaller domes. On the corners of the platform stand four lofty decorative minarets. And whether you see it shimmering in the moonlight or glistening proudly in the midday sun, whether you see it draped in the pink and gold of twilight or lit up brilliantly in artificial lamplight, the vision of splendour takes your breath away. More than the lovely formal garden around it, more than the perfectly planned reflection of the ethereal beauty sparkling in the silvery pool of water that stretches longingly out front, you are struck by the exquisite elegance of the monument itself. And you wonder how such amazing grace can be moulded out of hard, cold stone.

But Agra is more than the Taj. There is the Agra fort for one, an enormous structure dating back to the sixteenth century. It was here that Akbar made his fascinating decisions about religious tolerance and military might, it was here that

Reaching for the skies—the Qutb Minar stands 72.5 metres high. Built by Qutb-ud-din Aibak, it marked the beginning of Muslim rule in India in the late twelfth century.

Nurjahan read poems out to Jehangir, it was from one of the windows of the beautiful octagonal tower in this fort that the old Shah Jehan, imprisoned by his son Aurangzeb, stared wistfully at the Taj. Within the Agra fort is Shah Jehan's Pearl Mosque and his palace, with the ladies wing flaunting its own hall of mirrors called the Shish Mahal. Jehangir's palace, built by Akbar for his son, reflects in stone Akbar's 'Din-i-Ilahi' in the blending of Hindu and Muslim styles in architecture. Other sites of interest include Ram Bagh, the earliest Mughal garden, where Babur was buried till his remains were moved to Kabul, and the Jami Masjid, another of Shah Jehan's impressive creations.

Akbar's tomb is at SIKANDRA, near Agra. A tribute to religious syncretism, the four red sandstone gates of the tomb stand for Islam, Hinduism, Christianity and 'Din-i-Ilahi', the eclectic religion he created. The tomb itself combines Hindu and Muslim architectural patterns. A palace of Sultan Sikander Lodi, who lends his name to the town, stands in the garden surrounding Akbar's mausoleum.

FATEHPUR SIKRI, a small town near Agra, was the capital of the Mughal empire in Akbar's time, and seems remarkably well preserved. This is really the palace on the hilltop, the actual town at the foot of the hill having perished. Only its stone wall remains, protecting nothingness.

Akbar was blessed by Salim Chisti, a Muslim saint in Fatehpur Sikri, following which the emperor produced three sons; in gratitude he created this new capital. The Dargah Mosque, with its interplay of Hindu and Muslim patterns, is believed to be a copy of the holiest of holy mosques, the one in Mecca. The tomb of Salim Chisti lies in marble surroundings inside the mosque. Thousands throng to his *dargah* asking for the same favour he had granted the emperor 400 years ago.

Rambles through Rajputana

'The land of kings', Rajasthan is today a strange mix of ancient and royal grandeur and narrow, left-over dogma, that makes it as much the land of *sati* and caste

The Lotus Temple in Delhi, sanctum of the Baha'i faith, illuminated at night.

violence as of chivalry and valour. Huge forts dominate the region, throwing you back to the days of endless battles that these Kshatriyas prided themselves in. It flaunts a wonderful scenery, if you don't mind the great Thar desert, that is. And as if to defy the predominantly dry and arid landscape, the people are brilliantly decked in colourful saris, bright turbans and beautiful chunky jewellery.

The capital of Rajasthan is JAIPUR, the famed Pink City. The name is not unjustified if you take a quick look around. Most of the buildings in the Old City are made of pink sandstone. The city was built by Maharaja Jai Singh II in 1727, dutifully following the norms of the *Shilpa Shastra*, the ancient Hindu guidebook to architecture. The next year, however, Jai Singh had moved on from scriptural rules to the rules of the universe, and built the magnificent observatory, Jantar Mantar, a bigger and better version of the observatory he had built four years earlier in Delhi.

Wrapped in a wall with seven gates, the Old City is a wonderful sight, the brilliant colours of Rajput costumes adding to the soft film of pink that shimmers over the city and takes on a golden hue in the twilight hour. This ethereal charm centres

around the palace of the maharaja, in the heart of which lies the luxurious Chandra Mahal. Helpfully, the palace has been turned into a museum where you can get an idea of Rajputana's brave warriors, its bejewelled beauties and its well-nourished art and literary traditions, all under one roof. The other important house of history in Jaipur is the Central Museum in the Ram Niwas Gardens.

South of Jaipur is AJMER, an ancient town in the lap of greenery overlooking the Ana Sagar Lake and framed by hills. The *dargah* of a twelfth century Sufi saint, it is a major centre of pilgrimage for Indian Muslims. Built by Humayun, the shrine has a gate built by the Nizam of Hyderabad and two mosques built by Akbar and Shah Jehan. Some distance from the *dargah* are the ruins of a mosque built in two-and-a-half days by Mohammad Ghori when he invaded India in 1192. Ajmer, always a town of strategic importance, also has a fort built by Akbar, which houses the Ajmer museum. And a Jain temple that traces the progression of Jain mythology.

A view of the 'new' from the 'old': the scene from one of the minarets of Jama Masjid in Delhi. The high-rise buildings in the distance are part of New Delhi.

If there is a city in Rajasthan with more delicate splendour than the Pink City, it is UDAIPUR, the 'city of sunrise'. Built in 1567 by Maharana Udai Singh, believed to be a member of the Solar dynasty, this city on a lake is a stark contrast to the arid landscape of other cities of the state. Stashed with palaces of varying splendour, Udaipur's main attraction is Lake Pichola, the enormous spread of water with its picturesque islands hosting luxurious ancient palaces.

One of the oldest cities of Rajasthan, and the largest after Jaipur, is JODHPUR. Founded in 1459 by the Rajput king, Rao Jodha, this city has been immortalised in international parlance for a certain style of trousers once worn here, the horse-rider's breeches or 'jodhpurs'. But there is more to the city than a memory of tight pants. The old city is a labyrinth of narrow streets surrounded by a sixteenth century

Facing page: *The house of the President, the Rashtrapati Bhavan, is a 340-room palace in the centre of the country's capital, built as the residence of the viceroy in British India. After the change of guards in 1947, the ground reality is vastly different, but the palace continues to be the first address of the country.*

In the early seventeenth century, Nurjahan, the beautiful wife of Jehangir, built a mausoleum for her father Mirza Ghiyas Begh. The Itmad-ud-daulah in Agra set a new trend in Mughal architecture. The entire structure was carved out of marble, the arched windows were shaded by a delicate marble lattice-work, and the pattern on the pietra dura was exquisite. A few years later, this style was perfected in the Taj Mahal.

wall. Looming over the medieval city is the Meherangarh fort, a majestic statement of power standing on a hill.

The palaces inside the fort give a true flavour of Rajput royalty. Apart from a fantastic collection of paintings, musical instruments, furniture and costumes, they host an amazing assembly of armoury, cannons, palanquins and elephant *howdas*, bringing the maharajas of legends and fairy tales to life.

And no trip to Rajasthan can be complete without the golden city of JAISALMER. Dotted with exquisite mansions in soft amber sandstone, this city with a golden glow is like a dream town. Apart from the twelfth century hill-top fort, which flaunts a seven-storeyed palace, it houses *havelis* or luxury homes of the rich. It also has a number of beautiful Jain temples.

Apart from these royal retreats, Rajasthan has two of the most beautiful natural

Exquisite inlay work, marble screens, fine carvings and diffused light falling on the final resting place of Mumtaz Mahal.

parks. RANTHAMBHORE is a wildlife reserve, where tigers are the main attraction. BHARATPUR on the other hand is a bird sanctuary where migratory birds come in from around the world, and especially from Siberia. For a quiet holiday in the hills, go to MOUNT ABU, and for peace by the waterside, take a trip to PUSHKAR, the pretty town on the shores of Lake Pushkar. It helps to cool your heels after being subjected to the valour and vigour of Rajputana!

Himalayan Wonders

You don't need to be Tenzing Norgay to enjoy a sunrise in the Himalaya. You have a choice of lovely mountain resorts, and as long as diarrhoea is at bay, you have nothing to fear.

Kashmir was the summer retreat of the Mughal emperors, a land cradled by

Facing page: *The cenotaphs of Mumtaz Mahal and Shah Jahan surrounded by delicately perforated marble screens filled with translucent glass that filters the light. The Egyptian lamp hanging from the ceiling was presented by Lord Curzon.*

Silhouetted against the setting sun, the Taj Mahal acquires a soft, ephemeral glow, as night descends upon it.

majestic mountains and crafted out of scintillating lakes, magnificent fields of flowers and, of course, the usual spattering of ancient monuments. The Dal Lake in SRINAGAR, a patchwork of crystal-clear waterways with floating gardens, houseboats and ringed by the enticing Mughal gardens, had on its shore the Hazrat Bal Mosque (since then destroyed in a fire) where it is believed that a hair of the Prophet was preserved. The magnificence of nature reaches a crescendo in the valley of Kashmir. GULMARG, or the 'field of flowers' is a brilliant carpet of flowers in the summer, interrupted by cool pine forests.

One could move on to LEH, the trekkers' paradise, or to the less challenging treks in Kulu and Manali in Himachal Pradesh. The KULU valley stretches up to the Rohtang pass, that leads to Lahoul and Spiti, and down to the Beas river. It seems perpetually buzzing with activity, as women in silver jewellery and men in their special Kulu caps tend their orchards or dance to the beat of folk music during festivals. The queen of the valley is MANALI, known as much for its scenic beauty as its wild marijuana. SHIMLA, the capital of Himachal Pradesh and the summer capital of British India, is another all-time favourite.

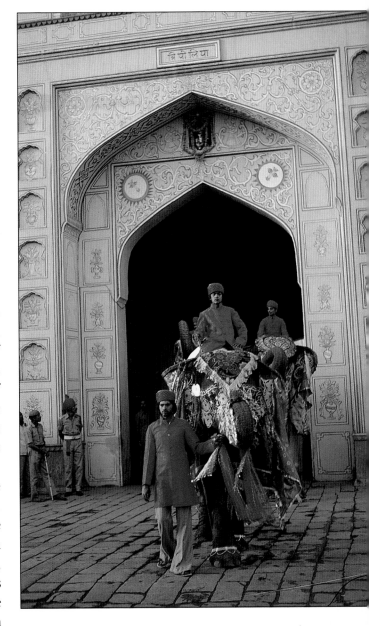

On a holier trip, you could go up to GANGOTRI, in Uttar Pradesh, and see the birthplace of the country's most sacred river, the Ganga. Further up is the actual glacier which melts to form the Ganga, visible from GOMUKH. A slightly more difficult trek is involved if you aim for YAMUNOTRI, the source of the holy waters of the Yamuna. But in spite of the flourishing temples, these pilgrimage centres have a lot more to offer than piety. Mountain springs and bubbling brooks breathe life into the chiselled perfection of snowcapped peaks, made even prettier by the rush of colourful orchids. Other places of Hindu worship nearby are KEDARNATH, with its astounding Shiva temple, and BADRINATH, the abode of Vishnu and one of the four holiest places India. The added attraction here is Alakananda, a river that has left its mark in Hindu mythology. And the Valley of Flowers is not too far, a virtual paradise in summer.

In the east, Sikkim is like a dream. And with predictable regularity the wonderstruck have called it Shangri-La. GANGTOK is the capital, a sleepy city bathed in silence and offering an exquisite view of the Kanchenjunga mountain. Home of the Nepalese, Tibetans, Lepchas, Bhutias and people from the Indian plains, Sikkim's culture is an odd mix of Buddhism and Hinduism, where very often the myths of one religion find representation in the forms of the other.

The closest to Gangtok in snowy splendour is DARJEELING, in the otherwise cramped state of West Bengal. Set in the soft greenery of tea plantations, and cradled by silvery-blue mountains, Darjeeling offers a magnificent view of the Kanchenjunga

A procession starting out from the Tripolia gate, the three-tiered entrance to the City Palace, Jaipur. Traditionally, all processions began and culminated at this gate.

Facing page: *Hawa Mahal—the pride of Jaipur. Its honeycomb structure is cleverly designed to invite the cool breeze while affording privacy to the royal ladies viewing state processions and activities on the street. It was built by Sawai Pratap Singh as a house of worship for Radha-Krishna in the 19th century.*

The beauty of glistening sands and the romantic ambience of Rajputana is best brought out by Jaisalmer. And amidst the splendour of this golden city stands the Jaisalmer fort, atop the Trikuta Hill. Built in the twelfth century, this sprawling fort hosts the royal palace where one finds the Satiyon ki Sidiyan, the steps leading the women towards jauhar to become satis.

as well. But for a truly fascinating view of sunrise in the Himalaya, you need to go up a little more, to Tiger Hill. And if you are lucky, you may even get to see Mt. Everest from there. Climbing down from Darjeeling, you get a totally different view of Himalayan life in KALIMPONG. It mixes bustling bazaars with peaceful Buddhist monasteries, and flaunts an incredible variety of flowers and orchids.

Calcutta

Between the alarming snarl of traffic, the grime and sweat of the crowds and the warm web of affection, CALCUTTA is a labyrinth of conflicting emotions where the individual is almost certain to lose his way. One of the world's largest cities, it is the home of 11 million people, most of whom suffer from a deep love-hate relationship with it. This is the cultural nerve-centre of India, the city of Rabindranath Tagore and Satyajit Ray, the city of poets and lovers. It is also the city of abject misery, where too many hands clutch at too few resources, where the streets are full of frustrated faces and homes full of memories of yesteryear. Once the capital of the British Raj, Calcutta is today an exhausted city.

Apparently Calcutta was a British creation. One noon in 1690, Job Charnock's ships swept down the Ganga and on to the shores of Sutanuti. And Charnock stayed, having put together the villages of Sutanuti, Govindapur and Kalikata, creating the capital of the British empire in India. Much later, another Briton would comment: *From the midday halt of Charnock/ More's the*

Chitrasala or the hall of paintings located in the Bundi Palace houses some of the best-known works seen in Rajasthan. Bundi palace is one of the finest examples of Rajput architecture.

Following pages: *The 17th century Jag Niwas is today known as the Lake Palace— one of the most romantic resorts in the world. At the lakeside is the City Palace, now converted into the Shiv Niwas Hotel.*

pity/ Grew a city,/ As fungus spreads chaotic/ From its bed/ So it spread/ Chance directed, chance erected/ Laid and Built/ On the silt/ Palace, pyre, hovel, poverty and pride/ Side by side... A century later, Rudyard Kipling's words seem prophetic.

The strongest reminder of Calcutta's lost stature is the Victoria Memorial. An imposing building of white marble, like a Taj Mahal that has put on weight, this tribute to British glory still symbolises the city. The dainty fairy that danced on the top of the dome has lost her step, and stares blankly at the green sweep of the *maidan* in the distance, her winged grace frozen in time. But the formidable queen magnificently guarding the building retains her posture, grim and royally unamused.

The other symbol of Calcutta is also a British construction, the Howrah Bridge. Built in 1943 over the Ganga, it is a wonder that this cantilevered bridge can still support a most astounding rush of daily traffic. Then there are trams, the hallmark

Jodhpur Fort, famous for its tales of valour and jauhar—the practice of wives choosing death over dishonour by jumping into a mass funeral pyre.

of Calcutta streets. And although they jam up the traffic and queue up helplessly on their tracks when there is a power failure, these electric coaches are a favourite with Calcuttans, and crawl round the city with great dignity if not speed.

The bigger colonial structures of Calcutta today mostly house various limbs of the communist government in West Bengal, and habits of the British Raj are kept alive only in two flagrantly opposing pockets of culture: in the posh clubs, where boxwallahs still rule, albeit in disguise, and in the Anglo-Indian community, flavoured by out-of-date dreams.

But these forgotten children of the British Raj are not the only ones who do not quite identify with the country yet belong solely to Calcutta. Tucked away in little corners of this bustling city are centuries-old legal aliens, like the Armenians and

Facing page: *Maharaj Gaj Singh II of Jodhpur (right), on the occasion of his birthday, with his son. Rising magnificently behind them, out of the rocky outcrops of a huge hill, is Meherangarh fort, sentinel of the Marwar empire.*

*There is a certain
charm in the golden
stretch of glistening
sand, especially if it
happens to constitute
one of the bigger
deserts of the world.
The Thar desert in
Rajasthan draws
thousands of tourists
each year, by dint of
its magical sands
alone. Well, maybe
with a little help from
the romance of
Rajputana.*

Z3 Zanskar (6270 m)

Nilkanth (6597 m)

Nanda Devi (7816 m)

Thalaisagar (6904 m)

Nandaghunti (6314 m)

Bhagirathi II, III, I (6512, 6454, 6856 m)

Shivling (6543 m)

Panwali Dhar (6663 m), Nanda Kot (6816 m)

the Chinese. With a fierce loyalty to their own customs, they live in their secluded worlds, shrugging off minor details of geography as they cling to their ancestral identities. And of course, the food in China Town is simply heavenly.

Whether it is in these little pockets of foreign culture or in the homes of the milling masses, tradition dominates Calcutta. It may have frayed at the edges, but it wraps around the housewife in her loosely looped sari and moulds into the clay cups of street-corner tea-shops. And it bursts into a thousand sparks during festive occasions like the Durga *puja* or Kali *puja*. But nowhere is tradition in daily life more pronounced than in the stately homes. And there are quite a few in Calcutta.

Tikse is one of the most attractive monasteries in Ladakh. It offers a respectable collection of art and Buddhist texts, apart from a lovely view of the Indus river.

Page 76:
Sunset over the 6543-metre tall Shivling peak in Garhwal. Named after the lingam *or phallus of Shiva which it is supposed to resemble, the sacred aura of the peak is heightened by the Ganges which rises in the surrounding area.*

The nineteenth century lives on in the Marble Palace or the Mullick House. A jumble of Indian and Western paintings, including original Rubens and Botticelli, marble Aphrodites and a huge shiny black Queen Victoria, the mansion reflects Raja Rajendra Mullick's passion for the arts as well as the unusual.

But the most revered of all mansions in Calcutta is Jorasanko's Thakur Badi, the home of the Tagores. This was the crux of Bengali culture in the pre-independence days, where Rabindranath Tagore learnt his alphabet, where his father, Devendranath, dreamt of a classless, casteless society, where his sister, Swarnakumari Devi, struggled for women's emancipation. It has seen the heights of affluence in the times of Rabindranath's grandfather, Prince Dwarakanath Tagore, a man of impeccable taste who is believed to have got all his laundry done from England via ocean liners. It has felt the rush of blood in its veins as the centre of Bengal's cultural renaissance. And it has cradled the movements against Brahminical Hinduism, with its vision of a society moulded out of liberty and

Facing page: *Festivities in Little Tibet, or Ladakh, almost always have a flavour of Buddhism at the folk level. The Hemis Festival is the most spectacular of them all. The backdrop is provided by a special* tankha, *an art-work of meticulous silk embroidery, that is brought out only on this festive occasion.*

A bird's-eye view of Calcutta cannot do justice to the city, moulded more out of emotion than concrete. It's fine to see the busy streets, the crowds, the imposing buildings that loom over the cramped city in a blinding colonial hangover. But for a clearer picture of this city of poetry and communism, one needs a view from the ground—for Calcutta is best experienced, let's say, at the grassroots level.

equality that was spearheaded by reformers like Ishwar Chandra Vidyasagar and Rammohan Roy.

This is the house where Rabindranath grew up with his thirteen siblings and a herd of cousins, where his nephews, Gaganendranath and Abanindranath, experimented with paint and changed the world of Indian art forever. Through the generations, members of this household had effortlessly redesigned Bengal's culturescape. But to the average Bengali, Jorasanko's Thakur Badi remains the sacred spot where Rabindranath was born and where he died. And Calcutta is

The Ganga, the most sacred river of India, seems to have washed away too many sins. Pollution has reached alarming levels and even the Howrah Bridge, which has been patiently hanging over the enormous breadth of the river with no support in the water for over 50 years, is endangered today.

probably the only city in India where a poet is worshipped with the same devotion as a saint. Tagore's birthday is celebrated with the pomp of a *puja*, only poetry and songs replace religious rituals. In this cosmopolitan city riddled with problems, the poet is still king.

But Rabindranath Tagore was not the only Nobel Laureate that Calcutta gifted to India. All four Nobel winners from India are from Calcutta. Tagore for literature, Sir C.V. Raman for physics, Mother Teresa for peace and Amartya Sen for economics. In fact there was a fifth Nobel Laureate from the city, an Englishman, Sir Ronald Ross, the pioneer of malaria research. But intellectual brilliance or dedication has very little to do with affluence, and Calcutta remains a shabbily garbed and withered city, its privations balanced comfortably by its intellectual wealth and emotional warmth.

The warmth of human sympathy was personified, till recently, by Calcutta's private hotline for the distressed—Mother Teresa. With the help of a host of devoted women, this missionary of charity dedicated her entire life to 'the poorest of the poor' and breathed new life into a city crawling with destitutes. Though no more, her homes for the aged, the disabled, the terminally ill, lepers and others shunned by society continue to bring hope and provide shelter to thousands, just as her orphanages give children the power to dream. And whether criticised for

Facing page: *The spirit of free India against a backdrop of the Victoria Memorial in Calcutta—symbol of British imperial glory.*

the rudimentary medical care she offered or charged with imposing Catholic values on a predominantly Hindu society, projected as gunning for sainthood or gunned down by politically correct Western liberals, Mother Teresa will remain a dearly loved mother-figure who Calcutta will always be proud of.

But the 'mother' that looms over the city's Hindu sentiments is Kali, the goddess of destruction. The temple at Kalighat, from where the city may have got its name, (Kalikata in Bengali) is one of the most sacred spots for Hindu pilgrims. Bustling with every conceivable religious activity, from quickie weddings to a barrage of prayers and thanksgivings, the temple throbs with a daily give and take of divine favours. This sacred business is much magnified in the Kali temple of Dakshineshwar, just north of Calcutta. Here, back in the nineteenth century, the rustic philospher Ramakrishna held endless dialogues (or so he believed) with his very own, very maternal 'Ma Kali', and was blessed with a vision after which he began to profess a unity of all religions.

Other sacred spots include the Nakhoda Masjid for Muslims and the St. Paul's Cathedral, an important place of worship for Indian Christians. The St. John's Church houses the tomb of the city's founder, Job Charnock. The other corridor to the past is the Park Street Cemetery, crowded with British names, dried leaves shrouding forgotten tombs. Some distance away is a Muslim burial ground. Wajid Ali Shah, the last Nawab of Oudh, lies buried in the Imambara Mosque, quite lost in the flurry of the city. For today, nostalgia isn't what it used to be.

On the Plains of the Ganga

A rather homely town at the base of the Himalaya, HARDWAR, where the Ganga spills out of the mountains and into the plains, is a sacred site for Hindus. Apart from the several bathing ghats offering to wash away your sins, this sprightly town clamouring with religious activity hosts lovely temples. But the beauty of the holy river blossoms further downstream, at Varanasi, or Benaras as it is more popularly known.

This is the Eternal City, the sacred ground where millions of Hindus have flocked through centuries for salvation. And through the ages VARANASI has also been a centre for learning. Brimming with piety and scholarship, this city of holy ghats is peppered with temples. But however beautiful they may be, the allure of a glorious past frozen in stone fades in comparison with the spectacular ghats, buzzing with religious souls taking their holy dip, saying their own little prayer or scrubbing their backs. The priests stand poised to bless, waiting to add their touch of Brahmin glory to your mundane non-Brahmin worship.

Next to the holy site for Hindus is SARNATH, a centre of pilgrimage for Buddhists. This is where Gautama Buddha first taught his message of inner peace. Further north is the birthplace of the Buddha, at LUMBINI in Nepal. And further east, in Bihar, is BODHGAYA, where he attained enlightenment. The precise spot of the Buddha's realisation of Truth is marked by the enormous Bodhi tree. More than 2,500 years ago, Gautama became the Buddha under the shade of a similar Bodhi tree from which a sapling was carried to Sri Lanka by Ashoka's son on his mission of spreading Buddhism. That sapling grew into a tree and has reigned over Buddhism in Sri Lanka for over twenty centuries. Later, when the Tree of Enlightenment in Bodhgaya died, a seed from the Sri Lankan Bodhi was planted here. Among the monasteries, the most sacred is the Mahabodhi Temple. There

Facing page: *The sacred act of praying with fire:* Aarati, *or honouring the gods with fire and* mantras *is one of the rituals in Hindu worship that can become an art.*

Holy flows the river along the holy city— the Ganges at Banaras, considered one of the most sacred cities for Hindus. The hustle and bustle of the pilgrims at the ghats dotted with bamboo umbrellas are a common, early morning sight.

are also Tibetan, Burmese, Japanese and Thai monasteries offering a bewildering variety of Buddhas.

Next to Bodhgaya is another holy spot for Hindus, GAYA. Pious Hindus prefer to ensure eternal peace for their forefathers by offering *pinda* here which is said to free departed souls from earthly bondage. And further east is PARASNATH, the spot where the twenty-third Jain Tirthankara attained enlightenment. One of the most important religious sites of the Jains, this little town on the top of a hill has twenty-four temples, each representing a Tirthankara.

But history overshadows religion in other parts of Bihar. Near the capital are the ruins of the Buddhist centre of learning at NALANDA, where the Chinese scholar and chronicler of the times, Hiuen Tsang, studied in the seventh century. The remains of stupas and parts of the school and library portray a vivid picture of the sprawling centre of Buddhism. On the banks of the Ganga is the capital of Bihar, PATNA. This city of contrasts was once Pataliputra, the capital of the huge Maurya empire in ancient India. And the remains of the city, dating back 2,300 years, complete with the fragments of its Buddhist monastery, add a different dimension to today's Patna, which rules over a casteist society where differences of opinion are settled with the gun. And ironically, the heart of the city is called the Gandhi Maidan.

The mineral-rich countryside makes way for the lush greenery of the lower Ganga plains in Bengal. Of the numerous pockets of tranquillity here, SANTINIKETAN is the most culturally active. The home of Tagore, this township was the hub of the new wave in Bengali literature and culture at one time. It houses Vishwa Bharati, the university founded by Devendranath Tagore, the poet's father, with a view to free the intellect and bring students closer to nature.

The call of the wild is best answered in the SUNDERBANS, the dense jungles in the deltas where the Ganga flows into the Bay of Bengal. The stars of these jungles are the Royal Bengal tigers, and crocodiles rule the waters, as more harmless beings like deer, monkeys and several birds try to live in peace. This place is no good for the beach-bum, but DIGHA is. Near the Orissa border, Digha is the only proper seaside resort in West Bengal with a fine stretch of beach and a lot of the tropical sun.

Beauty at Bay

The Indian peninsula offers a wide choice of beaches. On the east coast, the most famous beach resort is PURI in Orissa. Enormous waves throw themselves at the glistening sands, changing colour throughout the day. Peppered with seashells of all kinds, this remarkably clean beach is an all-time favourite, especially since one also gets to be blessed by Jagannath, the 'lord of the universe' who is cosily ensconced in his enormous temple.

In GOPALPUR, however, baywatching is the only attraction. Gopalpur-on-Sea is a quiet little place, with no pious crowd and only a steady trickle of upwardly-mobile beach-bums. Sliding further down the coastline, one comes to a lovely beach in Andhra Pradesh, WALTAIR. With its perfect combination of rocks and sand on the seaside, this is a popular resort for beachcombers.

The next important coast-stop is at MADRAS. The capital of Tamil Nadu, this large city wrapped in tradition was created by the British in the early seventeenth century, and later passed through the hands of the French as well. Today it is the

Facing page: *A temple on the banks of the Ganges that gets submerged regularly when the water rises. In the foreground, saris drying in the sun.*

fourth largest city of India. The aura of the past is mostly confined to Fort St. George, St. Mary's Church and a handful of historic temples, and the bustling centre of merchants three centuries ago is now a city of moderation, moderate climate, a balance of tradition and modernity, a busy city that is not quite manic. The Marina beach is not the best in the country but does offer a rather lengthy stretch of sands and sea for the desperate. Near it is the aquarium, which again is not too hot, but the Snake Park close by provides great amusement, even if you are not obsessed by cold-blooded reptiles. Then, of course, there is MAHABALIPURAM, flaunting a fine set of shore temples and a beautiful beach. The magnificent shore temples of the

Shiva, the lord of destruction, is believed to be rather dependent on his favourite bull, Nandi. As a result the divine bull has become quite a deity itself, revered from Kedarnath in the Himalaya to the various temples of south India.

seventh century, carved out of huge rocks, add to the splendour of the sea. The cave temples stand nearby.

The sea is rather lost at PONDICHERRY, famed as the 'little France' of India. The *ashram* of Rishi Aurobindo, Auroville, sprawls across the city, and thanks to Aurobindo's easily adaptable philosophy mixing Hindu and Western ideas, it draws devotees from across the world. All over Pondicherry, the French, who finally moved out a few years after independence, have left behind a large part of themselves in the names of roads, in the culture, in the uniform of the local police, in the language of the locals.

Near Pondicherry is PICHAVARAM, a lovely seaside haunt. The mangrove forest adds to the beauty, making this a small pocket of bliss in the backwaters. More sea-splendour lies further south, at RAMESWARAM—an island alive with temples and beaches, lined with cool coconut palms and magnificent coral reefs.

At the southern tip of the Indian peninsula lies KANYAKUMARI. Apart from offering a brilliant view, where the Bay of Bengal meets the Arabian Sea, it is also a holy spot for Hindus. Legend tells us that at this spot, the lovelorn Kanya, an incarnation of Parvati, had vowed to remain a virgin following her failed attempt at luring Lord Shiva into marriage. The arrangements of the cancelled wedding lay on the seaside for centuries, and turned into stone. The older generations still talk of the curious pebbles on the beach, shaped like rice and pulses and other essentials of a wedding feast. And off the shore, in a little island is the Vivekananda Rock, where Swami Vivekananda meditated in solitary peace a century ago.

For true splendour of the sea in coconut country you need to turn into the west coast, and get to KOVALAM in Kerala. With smooth cool rocks and swaying coconut palms, this resort is a favourite with those who love the sun and the surf. Just 12 kms north is THIRUVANANTHAPURAM, the capital of India's most literate state. Till recently named Trivandrum, this beautiful city nestles in the lap of greenery and seems to have as its main attraction its ancient temples, irrespective of the sentiments of Kerala's communist government. It also has its share of mosques and

The Gateway of India was constructed in 1911, to welcome King George V to his empire across the seas. The same occasion saw the birth of Jana gana mana adhinayaka jaya he' *Tagore's rather mysterious way of greeting the emperor. The song is today the national anthem of India, and the Gateway a landmark of Bombay.*

churches, since a quarter of the state's population is Christian and Muslims make up one-fifth.

Further north is KOCHI, the 'queen of the Arabian Sea'. A major port of Kerala and also known as Cochin, this lovely bit of land washed by the Arabian Sea is flush with historic monuments. The Portuguese church of St. Francis, dating back to the early 1500s, is the oldest European church in India. Scattered islands laced with palm trees enhance the beauty of this historic seaport. And the rich cultural fabric of mainland Ernakulam adds an intellectual edge to the grace of nature. Go up the costline and reach the spot where the first European settlers stepped ashore, KOZHIKODE. Also known as Calicut, this was where Vasco da Gama landed in 1498.

You don't find too many sea-resorts along the coast of Karnataka. But then you come to what is undoubtedly the best stretch of beaches in the country, GOA. Till 1961, Goa was under Portuguese rule. And it certainly shows. The influence lives on in the customs, cultural habits and cuisine of the land, not to mention the excellent Portuguese wines. But it is not just the European ambience in the tropics of India that draws one million tourists to Goa every year. The spectacular beaches that exude a *joie de vivre* have a role. The Basilica of Bom Jesus in Old Goa, which houses the mortal remains of St. Francis Xavier (the body is said to have remained intact for more than 400 years!), the Assisi Church and the Se Cathedral are of

special interest to Christians. But nothing compares with the splendour of the Goan beaches.

Colva is probably the best, with its endless stretch of silvery sands along the warm clear sea, fringed by coconut palms. The Calangute beach is pretty much the same, only more crowded with foreign sun-bathers, punks and fun-seeking freaks of all kinds. These are tiny pockets of freedom for the middle class Indian tourist who can stretch out on the sand and sip on some port wine or *feni* (the local produce), can dance to the Portuguese-Indian music and shamelessly watch bikini-clad foreign tourists but still not feel guilty.

Charminar, looming over Hyderabad city, was constructed in the sixteenth century to mark the end of a plague that ravaged the area.

The first city of Indian business and the capital of Maharashtra, BOMBAY is a large island on the Arabian Sea. But it does not feel like an island, and certainly does not flaunt the idyllic beauty that islands have been known to offer. It is a fast-paced business centre, more washed by money than by sea-waves. The Gateway of India has lost its value with air travel taking the place of ocean liners. Bombay may not be the only welcome point for foreigners anymore, but it remains the main port of India. The Colaba Causeway is a fascinating mix of fishermen, tourists, junkies and officegoers, bringing out the intrinsic attraction of this immensely cosmopolitan city. The Marine Drive along the shoreline gives a fine view of the sea and the Chowpatty beach never ceases to amaze with its beach-bums and sandcastles and jumble of curious activities. At one end of Marine Drive is Malabar Hill, the Beverly Hills of India, at the other is Nariman Point, the ever-bustling business centre. The other business centre is at Flora Fountain.

The Tower of Silence, where the Parsis lay out their dead, St. John's Church, the Cathedral of St. Thomas, Haji Ali's mosque and the Mahalaxmi temple add the

Facing page: *In the eighteenth century, Sultan Hyder Ali started building this palace in Mysore, but between the tense fighting with the British and assorted nationalistic concerns, he could not complete it. His son, Tipu Sultan, who carried on Hyder Ali's struggle, gave the palace its final shape.*

religious touch to this otherwise trade-centric city. And the Hanging Gardens, the Victoria Gardens and the aquarium provide the element of peace and beauty amidst the hectic activity. The glamour of 'Bollywood', the fond name for the tinsel town where the enormous Indian film industry thrives, the screams of the stock market, the cheap lipstick in the alleys of sin mingle with the rush of sweaty commuters and flashy cars in this frantic city. It is the most moneyed city in the country, as well as the city that houses Asia's biggest slum, Dharavi.

Further north, in Gujarat, the sea seems to have lost its charm. Although DAMAN has a number of beaches, it lacks the magnificence of Goa. The best feel of the sea

In a country thriving on myths, this piece of hard rock in Mahabalipuram, Tamil Nadu, is known, ironically, by the tender name of Krishna's Butter.

in this region is probably at DIU. This tiny island, which with Daman and Goa formed the Portuguese colony in India, sports lovely retreats with warm sands and a relatively clear sea. Memories of the Portuguese lie scattered along its streets, churches and in the sixteenth century fort.

The land of myths and legends, DWARKA is a holy site for Hindus, with various temples of Lord Krishna. Another city which devotees flock to is PORBANDAR, the birthplace of Mahatma Gandhi. On the whole the attraction of sun-drenched sands and the cliffs of sea-resorts ends with the fabulous beaches of Goa.

There is a lot more to India's beauty. The most important relates to the saying about the eyes of the beholder. So look beyond the obvious. You never know what you may find. After all, this is India.

Facing page: *At the annual Khajuraho festival, India's best dancers bring alive their centuries-old tradition, reflected in the stone sculptures.*